AMERICAN KERNEL LESSONS

AKL: BEGINNING

ROBERT O'NEILL
LARRY ANGER AND KAREN DAVY

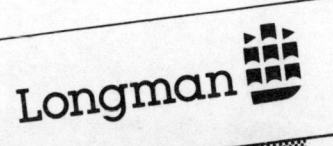

American Kernel Lessons: Beginning

Library of Congress Cataloging in Publication Data

O'Neill, Robert.
   American Kernel Lessons: Beginning
   Includes index.
   1. English language—Textbooks for foreigners.
I. Anger, Larry.   II. Davy, Karen.   III. Title.
PE1128.05   428.2'4   81-1365
                 AACR2

ISBN 0-582-79734-9

Copyright © 1981, by Longman Inc. All rights reserved. No part of this book or related recordings may be reproduced, stored in a retrieval system or transmitted in any form or means, electronic, mechanical, photocopying, recording or otherwise, without prior permission from the publisher.

First printing 1981

5   4   3

Cover Design: Frederick Charles Ltd.
Cover Photography: Ken Karp
Character Illustrations: John Walsh and M. J. Quay
Design: Robert Fitzpatrick/Flex, Inc.

We wish to thank the following for providing us with photographs: Page 2, top: Derek Long; center: Lemar Morrison (photo 1); New York Convention and Visitors Bureau (photos 2, 3, 4). Page 6, top: Derek Long; bottom: American Airlines; Trans World Airlines; Braniff International; United Airlines. Page 8: American Airlines; Derek Long. Page 10: Derek Long. Page 29, top: Angel L. Cuevas; bottom: Lemar Morrison (photos 1, 4); Greater Los Angeles Visitors and Convention Bureau (photo 2); New York University (photo 3). Page 89: Hardwicke Companies Incorporated. Page 96: Derek Long. Page 105: Derek Long. Page 109: New York Convention and Visitors Bureau. Page 110: New York City Transit Authority.

Thanks also to the following artists: Audrey Sclater for the maps on pages 3, 31 and 107. Anna Veltfort for the map on page 109 and the illustrations on page 110. Gregory Stewart for the illustrations on page 18.

Special thanks to Nancy Perry for all her help.

Longman Inc.
19 West 44th Street
New York, New York 10036

Distributed in the United Kingdom by Longman Group Ltd., Longman House, Burnt Mill, Harlow, Essex CM20 2JE, England, and by associated companies, branches and representatives throughout the world.

Printed in Singapore

ACKNOWLEDGEMENTS

Two people have collaborated directly on certain aspects of the material: Alan McLean on the Reading and Writing Follow-Ups, and David Mills on the Review, Word List and Verb List. They also gave me valuable advice and criticism while the material was being written.

There were many other people who helped me in various phases of the conception and execution of this book. I would like to mention Waldo Bindseil, Gareth Thomas, Ros Hurst and Erhard Waespi of Eurocentres. My gratitude is also extended to the staffs of Longman Group Ltd. and Longman Inc.

Robert O'Neill, 1981

CONTENTS

Unit 1   HI 1
What's your name?
What time is it?
Where are you from?

Unit 2   ON THE PLANE 5
Where are you going?
I'm going to New York.
Is this/that your suitcase?

Unit 3   ON THE TRAIN 9
What are they doing?
What time is her train?
How much is his ticket?

Unit 4   IN NEW YORK 13
We're over New York now.
I can see the Empire State Building.
Can you see the picture on the left/right?

Unit 5   AT THE AIRPORT 17
Harry and Jackie have their suitcases now.
What do you have in your suitcase?
She doesn't have an umbrella.

Unit 6   A ROOM FOR THE NIGHT 23
There is a chair in his room.
There are two windows in her room.
Jackie can see Central Park from her window.
   What can Mike see?
How many doors are there in the classroom?

READING AND WRITING FOLLOW-UP:
   Units 1–6 29

Unit 7   A JOB IN GREENWICH VILLAGE 31
Can you type?
How many languages can you speak?

Unit 8   MONDAY MORNING 37
Carol lives in Rye. She works in Greenwich
   Village.
Where do you live?

Unit 9   WATCHING JACKIE 43
She always gets up at 7:00.
She usually leaves at 8:30.
What time do you get up?
When does she watch television?
Do you come here often?

READING AND WRITING FOLLOW-UP:
   Units 7–9 49

Unit 10   THE BURGLAR 51
There's a man in Bill's apartment.
I don't know him. He doesn't live there.

Unit 11   FRIDAY EVENING 57
Do you like pizza?
I don't want any wine.
I'd like a glass of water.
Do you want some coffee?

Unit 12   SATURDAY MORNING 63
What do you want to do tonight?
Let's go to a movie.

READING AND WRITING FOLLOW-UP:
   Units 9–12 69

Unit 13   FRANK'S LAST DAY IN PRISON 71
He was in prison yesterday.
Where were you last year?

Unit 14   CAROL'S OLD JOB 77
Carol worked in an office last year. Where did you
   work?

Unit 15   A JOB FOR FRANK 83
He got up at 7:00 yesterday.
He went to an interview.
What did you do yesterday?

READING AND WRITING FOLLOW-UP:
   Units 13–15 89

Unit 16   THE KIDNAPPING 91
Mike didn't see Jackie yesterday. Why didn't she
   come to the movie theater?

Unit 17   THE TELEPHONE CALL 97
Is Jackie going to see her father again?
What are they going to do to her?

Unit 18   A MILLION DOLLARS! 103
Mr. Hunter has to find a million dollars.
What does he have to do then?

READING AND WRITING FOLLOW-UP:
   Units 16–18 109

Unit 19   GOODBYE 111
What happened at the factory?
Did they free Jackie?
What about Lucky?

Review 117

Days, Months, Numbers 125

Verb List with Past Tense Forms 125

Word List 127

UNIT 1
Hi

1a

1.
BILL: Hi. My name's Bill Rivera.
SUE: Hello. My name is Sue Peterson.

2.
BILL: What's your name?
SUE: Sue Peterson. What's your name?
BILL: Bill Rivera.
SUE: Nice to meet you, Bill.
BILL: Nice to meet you too.

3.
BILL: Hey, Sue?
SUE: Yes?
BILL: What time is it?
SUE: It's one o'clock. See?
BILL: Thank you.

4.

0 1 2 3
   4 5 6

Zero   One   Two   Three
   Four   Five   Six

1b

1 Ask and answer the question.

What time is it?   It's (It is) ___ o'clock.

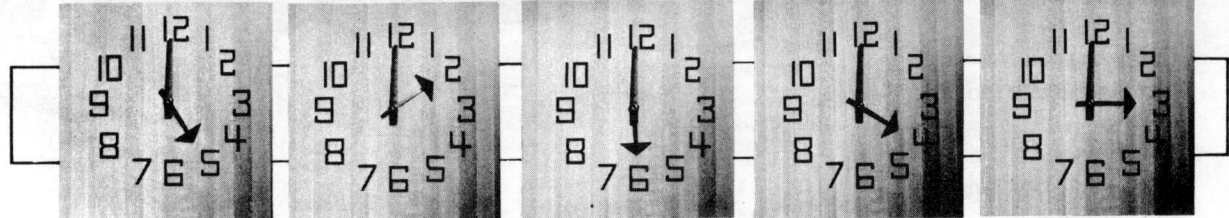

2 Look at the four pictures. LISTEN

PICTURE ONE
This is San Francisco.
San Francisco is a city.
It's in California.
California is a state.
San Francisco, California
is in the United States.

PICTURE TWO
And this is New York.
New York is a city too.
It isn't in California.
It's in New York.
New York, New York is in
the United States.

PICTURE THREE
This is the Empire State Building.
It's in New York.

PICTURE FOUR
And this is Fifth Avenue.
Fifth Avenue is a street in New York.

3 Ask and answer the questions.

Is ___ in ___?   Yes, it is.
                 No, it isn't.

Is New York in the United States?   Yes, it is.

1. ___ San Francisco in the United States?   Yes, it ___.
2. ___ San Francisco in California?   Yes, it ___.
3. ___ New York in California?   No, it ___.
4. ___ the Empire State Building in New York?   ___, ___ ___.
5. ___ the Empire State Building ___ San Francisco?   ___, ___ ___.
6. ___ Fifth Avenue a street ___ New York?   ___, ___ ___.
7. ___ Fifth Avenue a street ___ San Francisco?   ___, ___ ___.

1c

1 Look at the map. 🎧

The United States is a country.

California is a state and Texas is a state too.

San Francisco is a city in California. Los Angeles is in California too.

Dallas is a city in Texas. Houston is in Texas too.

Where is Miami? Where is Chicago? And where is Boston?

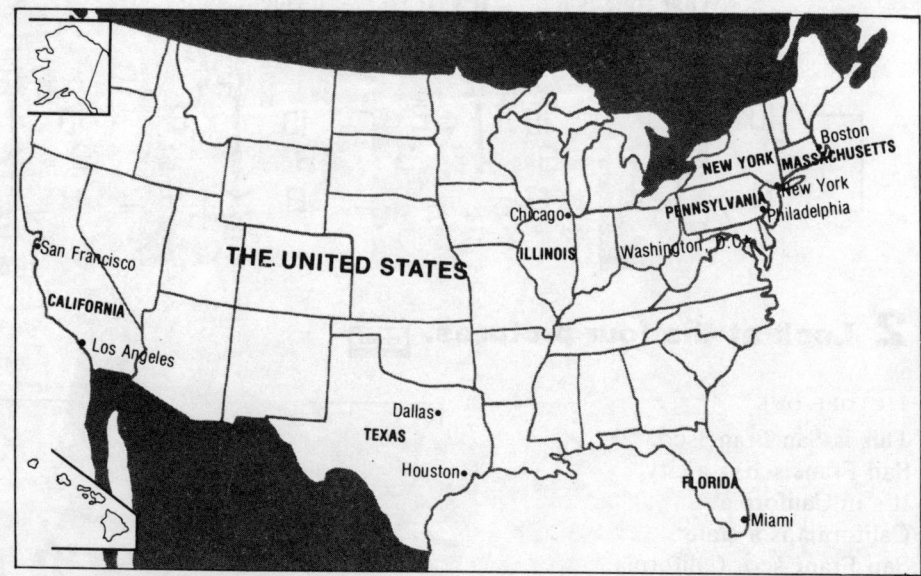

2 Ask and answer the question.

Where's (Where is) ___?   It's (It is) in ___.

3 Look at Sue and Bill. 🎧

Sue is in New York.
Bill is in New York too.

Bill isn't from New York.
He's from Dallas, Texas.

What about Sue?
She's from Los Angeles, California.

4 Ask and answer the questions.

Is	Bill Sue	in from	the United States? New York? California? Texas? Los Angeles? Dallas?	Yes, No,	he she he she	is. isn't.

1d

1 LISTEN

BILL: Where are you from, Sue?
SUE: Excuse me?
BILL: Where are you from?
SUE: Los Angeles.
BILL: Oh, really?
SUE: Yes. Where are you from?
BILL: I'm from Dallas.
SUE: Oh.

2 Open Dialog: Choose a partner and complete the conversation.

BILL: What's ___ name?
YOU: ___ name's ___.
BILL: Where are ___ from?
YOU: Excuse me?
BILL: Where ___ ___ ___?
YOU: Oh, I'm from ___.

3 Look at the grammar: BE

YOU SAY AND WRITE:

I	'm
You	're
He / She / It	's

YOU CAN ALSO WRITE:

I	am
You	are
He / She / It	is

4 Write is, am, are, He, She, It, in **or** from.

The United States *is* a country.

1. The Empire State Building ___ in New York.
2. Bill Rivera is ___ New York.
3. ___ is ___ Dallas.
4. Sue Peterson ___ from Los Angeles.
5. ___ is in New York.
6. New York ___ a city.
7. ___ is in the United States.

5 What about you?

1. Where ___ you from?
2. I ___ from ___.
3. My name ___ ___ ___.

UNIT 2
On the Plane

2a

LISTEN

1

This is Jackie Hunter.
She is on a street in San Francisco.
A taxi is coming.
It is seven o'clock.

JACKIE: Taxi! Taxi!

2

She is in the taxi now.

TAXI DRIVER: Where to?
JACKIE: The airport, please.

3

Where is the taxi going?
It is going to San Francisco Airport.
Where is Jackie going?
She is going to San Francisco Airport.

4

And this is San Francisco Airport.
Look! A plane is coming from New York.

5

Now Jackie is at San Francisco Airport.

JACKIE: Good morning. I'm going to New York.
TICKET AGENT: Your ticket, please.
JACKIE: Here you are.
TICKET AGENT: Is this your suitcase?
JACKIE: No, that's my suitcase.
And that's my suitcase too.

5

Answer the questions.

Yes,	he she it	is.	No,	he she it	isn't.

PICTURE ONE

1. Is Jackie in New York?
2. Is she in California?
3. Is she in San Francisco?
4. Is a taxi coming?

PICTURE TWO

1. Is Jackie in the taxi?
2. Is the taxi driver in the taxi too?

PICTURE THREE

1. Is Jackie going to San Francisco Airport?
2. Is the taxi going to San Francisco Airport?

PICTURE FOUR

1. Is this New York Airport?
2. Is it San Francisco Airport?
3. Look at the plane. Is it going to New York?
4. Is it coming from New York?

PICTURE FIVE

1. Is Jackie in the taxi?
2. Is she going to the airport?
3. Is she at the airport?
4. Is she going to New York?

2b

1 Ask and answer the question.

What time is it?   It's ___ o'clock.

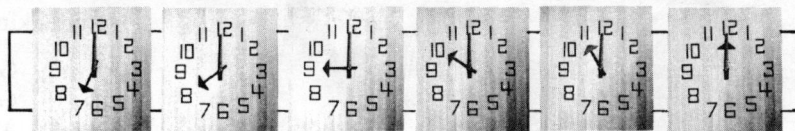

7	8	9	10	11	12
Seven	Eight	Nine	Ten	Eleven	Twelve

2 Open Dialog

TICKET AGENT: Is this your ___?
YOU: No, it isn't.
That's my ___.

coat — book — newspaper
bag — camera — briefcase

3 Ask and answer the questions.

Is the plane { going to ....? / coming from ....? }

Where is it { going? / coming from? }

1
San Francisco → New York

2
Dallas ← Los Angeles

3
Dallas → New York

4
New York → Los Angeles

2c

1

And now look at this man. His name is Harry Gilmore.
Harry is in San Francisco too. He is at a hotel.
Harry is from New York.
He is talking to a clerk.

CLERK: Good morning, Mr. Gilmore.
HARRY: Good morning. Call me a taxi, please.
CLERK: A taxi? Yes, sir.

2

It is seven fifteen now.

CLERK: Mr. Gilmore! Your taxi is here.
HARRY: Thank you.
CLERK: Is that your suitcase?
HARRY: Yes, it is. Where's the porter?
CLERK: The porter's coming sir.

3

Listen to Harry and the taxi driver.

TAXI DRIVER: Where are you going?
HARRY: San Francisco Airport.
TAXI DRIVER: San Francisco Airport? OK. Get in.

4

It is eight fifteen now and Harry is at San Francisco Airport.

TICKET AGENT: Where are you going, sir?
HARRY: I'm going to New York. Here's my ticket.
TICKET AGENT: Thank you. And where's your suitcase?
HARRY: Here.
TICKET AGENT: Put it right here, please. Thank you, sir.

2d

PICTURE ONE

1. Look at the man. What is his name?
2. Where is he from?
3. Where is he now?
4. Is he talking to Jackie Hunter?

PICTURE TWO

1. What time is it?
2. Is the taxi here?
3. Is Harry in the taxi?
4. Is the porter coming?

PICTURE THREE

1. Is Harry at San Francisco Airport now?
2. Is he on a street in San Francisco?
3. Where is he going?
4. Where is the taxi driver?

PICTURE FOUR

1. Where is Harry now?
2. What time is it?
3. Is Harry going to Dallas?
4. Where is he going?

1

It is nine fifteen now. Jackie Hunter and Harry Gilmore are on a plane. The plane isn't coming from New York. It is going to New York.

Ask and answer the questions.

1. ___ the plane going to San Francisco? No, it ___.
2. Where is it ___? It is ___ to New York.
3. ___ Jackie ___ to New York? Yes, ___ is.
4. ___ Harry ___ to New York too? Yes, ___ ___.

2 Open Dialog

TICKET AGENT: Where ___ ___ going, sir?
HARRY: I'm ___ to New York.
TICKET AGENT: ___ ticket, please.
HARRY: Here ___ are.
TICKET AGENT: Thank ___. And ___ that ___ suitcase?
HARRY: No, ___ ___. This ___ ___ suitcase.

3 Say the numbers.

13 **14** **15** **16** **17** **18**
Thirteen Fourteen Fifteen Sixteen Seventeen Eighteen

4 Write the sentences.

A taxi ___ coming. *A taxi is coming.*

1. Harry ___ in a taxi.
2. He ___ ___ to San Francisco Airport.
3. Jackie is ___ a taxi too.
4. ___ is ___ to San Francisco Airport too.
5. And now ___ ___ nine fifteen.
6. Jackie is on ___ plane.
7. She is going ___ New York.
8. Harry is on the ___ too.
9. ___ is going to ___ ___ too.

8

UNIT 3
On the Train

3a

This is South Station.
It is a big station in Boston.
Look at track four. The train to
New York is on track four.
That is the eleven forty-five train
to New York.

Look at this man and this woman.
His name is Mike Brodsky and her
name is Carol Lee. They are not
in New York. They are in Boston.
Look at the time. It is eleven
thirty-five. Mike and Carol are
late. They are running.

Carol Lee is asking about the train to Rye.

CAROL: What time is the train to Rye?
CLERK: Eleven forty-five.
CAROL: And what track is it on?
CLERK: Track four.
CAROL: Thank you.

Mike Brodsky is buying a ticket.

MIKE: A ticket to New York, please.
CLERK: One-way or round trip?
MIKE: Oh, one way.
CLERK: That's twenty-nine dollars and fifty cents.
MIKE: Excuse me? How much is it?
CLERK: Twenty-nine fifty.

3b

Answer the questions.

PICTURE ONE

1. Where is South Station?
2. Is it a big station?
3. Where is the eleven forty-five train to New York?

PICTURE TWO

1. Look at that man. What is his name?
2. Look at that woman. What is her name?
3. Where are they?
4. What are they doing?

PICTURE THREE

1. What is Carol doing now?
2. What time is her train?

PICTURE FOUR

1. What is Mike buying?
2. Where is he going?
3. How much is his ticket?

1 Say the numbers.

19	20	21	30	32	40
Nineteen	Twenty	Twenty-one	Thirty	Thirty-two	Forty

43	50	54	60	65
Forty-three	Fifty	Fifty-four	Sixty	Sixty-five

2 Ask and answer the question.

Excuse me. What time is it?   It's ___ ___.

3 Open Dialog

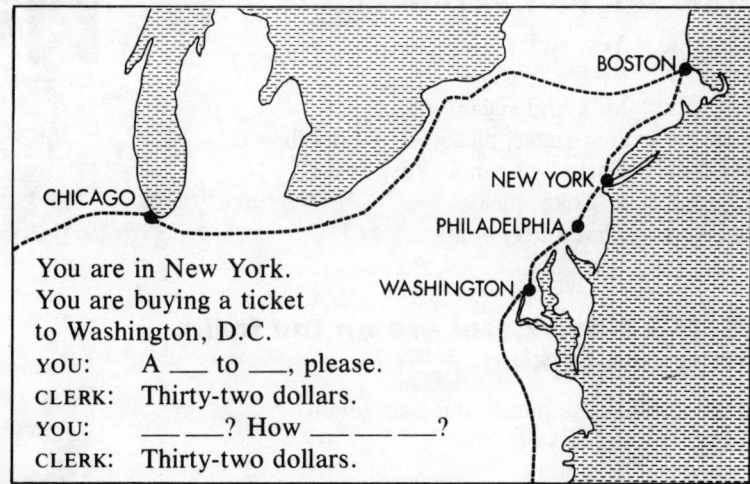

You are in New York.
You are buying a ticket to Washington, D.C.

YOU: A ___ to ___, please.
CLERK: Thirty-two dollars.
YOU: ___ ___? How ___ ___ ___?
CLERK: Thirty-two dollars.

4 Ask and answer the questions.

What time is the train to ___?
What track is it on?
How much is a ticket to ___?

DESTINATION	TRACK	TIME	FARE
Washington	9	6:40	$32.00
Chicago	14	7:15	$61.00
Boston	7	8:20	$29.50
Philadelphia	12	9:30	$14.25

3c

1 LISTEN

It is eleven forty-five and the train is leaving. It is going to New York. Carol and Mike are on the train. They are leaving Boston. He is going to New York and she is going to Rye. Rye is near New York.

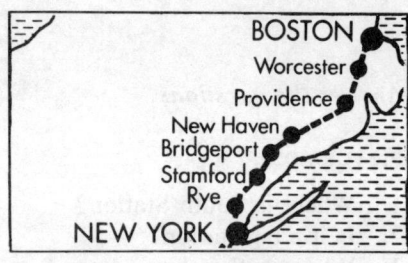

2 Ask and answer the questions.

1. What time ___ ___?
2. Where ___ ___ train going?
3. ___ Mike on ___ train?
4. ___ Carol ___ ___ train too?
5. Where ___ she going?
6. ___ Mike ___ to Rye too?
7. Where ___ ___ going?
8. Where ___ Rye?

3 This is the snack bar on the train. Mike and Carol are in the snack bar. What are they buying? LISTEN

WAITER: Yes, sir?
MIKE: Coffee, please.
WAITER: Milk and sugar?
MIKE: Just sugar, please. How much is it?
WAITER: Forty-five cents. Yes, miss?
CAROL: A Coke, please.
WAITER: That's fifty cents.

4 Mike and Carol are on the train. They are talking. LISTEN

CAROL: Excuse me. Is this seat taken?
MIKE: No, it isn't.
CAROL: Oh, good.
MIKE: Cigarette?
CAROL: No, thank you.
MIKE: Where are you going?
CAROL: To Rye.
MIKE: Oh. I'm going to New York.

5 Ask and answer the questions.

Are Carol and Mike on a train?   Yes, they are.
Are they on a plane?   No, they aren't.

1. ___ Carol and Mike leaving New York?
2. Are ___ leaving Boston?
3. ___ ___ going to Chicago?
4. ___ ___ talking?

3d

1 This is the menu in the snack bar. Ask and answer the question.

How much is ....?
.... is ....

```
MENU
COFFEE/TEA    45¢
SODA          50¢
BEER          85¢
     SANDWICHES
ROAST BEEF    $1.75
HAM & CHEESE  $1.50
EGG SALAD     $1.25
TUNA FISH     $1.25
```

2 Open Dialog

You are buying coffee and a roast beef sandwich.

WAITER: Yes, ___?
YOU: ___ and a ___ ___ ___, please.
WAITER: That's ___ ___, please.
YOU: ___ much ___ ___?
WAITER: Two twenty.

And now you are talking to Mike.

YOU: Excuse ___. Is this seat ___?
MIKE: No, ___ ___.
YOU: Where ___ you ___?
MIKE: I'm ___ to New York. Where ___ ___ ___?
YOU: ___ ___ to New York too.

3 Look at the grammar: Present Progressive

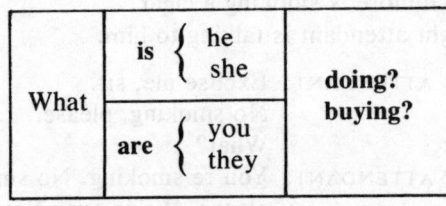

| What | is { he / she } are { you / they } | doing? buying? |

I am		
He / She is	buying	a sandwich. coffee.
They are		

YOU SAY AND WRITE:

I'm	
He / She / It 's	going
You / They 're	

YOU CAN ALSO WRITE:

I am	
He / She / It is	going
You / They are	

4 Write her, His, My, is, am, going, I, He or she.

This man and this woman are on a train.
___ name ___ Mike Brodsky and ___ name ___ Carol Lee. ___ is ___ to New York and ___ is ___ to Rye. They are talking.

MIKE: ___ name ___ Mike Brodsky.
       ___ ___ going to New York.
CAROL: ___ name ___ Carol Lee.
       ___ ___ ___ to Rye.

UNIT 4
In New York

4a

This is New York.
It is five o'clock in the afternoon and it is raining.
Can you see that plane up there?
Jackie Hunter and Harry Gilmore are on it.
They are coming from San Francisco.

Jackie can see the Empire State Building.
She is talking to a woman.

JACKIE:	We're over New York now.
WOMAN:	Are we?
JACKIE:	Yes. I can see the Empire State Building. Look down there!
WOMAN:	Oh, yes. I can see it too. Is it raining?
JACKIE:	Yes, it is.

Harry Gilmore is smoking a cigar.
The flight attendant is talking to him.

FLIGHT ATTENDANT:	Excuse me, sir. No smoking, please.
HARRY:	What?
FLIGHT ATTENDANT:	You're smoking. No smoking, please. We're over New York. We're landing.

What about Mike Brodsky and Carol Lee?
They are in Rye now and it's raining there too. Mike is on the train and Carol is on the platform.

MIKE:	Well, goodbye, Carol. Here's your suitcase.
CAROL:	Thanks, Mike. Goodbye.

4b

1 Say and write these sentences.
Use He, She **or** They.

Jackie is on a plane. *She is on a plane.*

Jackie and Harry are on a plane. *They are on a plane.*

1. Mike and Carol are in Rye.
2. Carol is from Rye.
3. Mike is on the train.
4. Carol is on the platform.
5. Bill and Sue are in New York.
6. Sue is from Los Angeles.
7. Bill is from Dallas.
8. Jackie and Sue are from California.

2 Look at the grammar: Review

I	am	
He / She / It	is	in San Francisco. going to New York.
You / We / They	are	

3 Open Dialog

You are on the plane to New York and you are talking to the flight attendant.

YOU: Excuse ___. ___ we over New York now?
FLIGHT ATTENDANT: Yes, ___ are. And ___ landing.
YOU: ___ ___ raining?
FLIGHT ATTENDANT: Yes, ___ ___.
YOU: And ___ time ___ ___, please?
FLIGHT ATTENDANT: It's five ___.
YOU: Thank ___.

PICTURE ONE

1. *Talk about the picture. Say:*
   I can see............. .
2. *Ask questions about the picture. Say:*
   Can you see ___ ___?
   ___ **time** ___ ___?
3. *Now answer the questions.*

PICTURE TWO

1. Where is Jackie now?
2. Is Harry on the plane too?
3. What can Jackie see?
4. Is it raining?

PICTURE THREE

1. Is the flight attendant smoking?
2. Is Harry smoking?
3. What is he smoking?
4. Is the plane landing now?
5. Where is it landing?

PICTURE FOUR

Ask and answer the questions.

1. Where ___ Mike ___ Carol?
2. Is ___ on the ___?
3. ___ ___ raining ___ Rye too?
4. Mike is saying:
   "Well, goodbye, Carol. Here's your suitcase."
   What is Carol saying?

14

4c

1 LISTEN

Here are two pictures. One picture is on the left. The other picture is on the right.

In the picture on the left, you can see Kennedy Airport in New York. In the other picture, you can see Grand Central Station. Grand Central Station is a big train station in New York.

You can see a plane and a train in the pictures. The plane and the train are arriving in New York. Is the plane on the left? Is the train on the left? Where is the train?

2 Ask and answer the questions.

Is the ___ on the ___?   Where is the ___?

3 You can hear two announcements. LISTEN

ANNOUNCER ONE: The eleven forty-five train from Boston is now arriving on track twelve.

ANNOUNCER TWO: American Airlines announces the arrival of Flight fifty-three from San Francisco.

4 Answer the questions.

1. What can you see in the picture on the left?
2. What can you see on the right?
3. Where is Grand Central Station?
4. Is the train arriving at Grand Central Station?
5. Which track is it arriving on?
6. Is it coming from Chicago?
7. Where is it coming from?
8. And what about the plane? Where is it coming from?

5 Write the sentences.

This ___ Grand Central ___. ___ track ___ ___ right is track twelve. ___ train ___ Boston is arriving ___ track ___.

Mike Brodsky ___ ___ ___ train. Jackie Hunter ___ on the train. She ___ ___ the plane ___ San Francisco. The plane is ___ at Kennedy Airport.

4d

1 Mike Brodsky is calling Bill Rivera now.

MIKE: Two-five-four, three-nine-seven-oh.
BILL: Hello?
MIKE: Hello. Is this Bill Rivera?
BILL: Yes, it is. Who's this?
MIKE: It's Mike.
BILL: Who?
MIKE: Mike Brodsky.
BILL: Mike! Where are you?
MIKE: I'm at Grand Central Station.
BILL: Grand Central Station?
MIKE: That's right. I'm in New York!

2 Open Dialog

Now you are calling Bill Rivera. You are at Kennedy Airport.

BILL: Hello?
YOU: Hello. Is ___ Bill Rivera?
BILL: Yes, ___ ___.
YOU: Hi, Bill. ___ ___.
BILL: Who?
YOU: ___ ___.
BILL: ___! Where ___ you?
YOU: ___ ___ Kennedy Airport.
BILL: Kennedy Airport?
YOU: ___ right. ___ ___ New York!

3 Complete the questions and answers.

<u>Is this</u> Sue? Yes, <u>it is</u>.

And <u>who's this</u>?
<u>It's</u> Mike.

1. ___ ___ Jackie?
   Yes, ___ ___.

2. And ___ ___?
   ___ Carol.

3. ___ ___ Harry?
   Yes, ___ ___.

4. And ___ ___?
   ___ Bill.

UNIT 5
At the Airport

5a

The passengers on Flight 53 from San Francisco are at Kennedy Airport now. Jackie and Harry and the other passengers are waiting for their suitcases. Their suitcases are coming now. Harry is wearing a coat and hat. What about Jackie?

Harry and Jackie have their suitcases now. Harry has one suitcase and Jackie has two suitcases. Jackie is walking with a porter. He is carrying her suitcases.

This man is at Kennedy Airport. His name is Pat.
He is wearing an old coat and he is carrying an umbrella.
Pat doesn't have a suitcase and he doesn't have a ticket either.
A policewoman is looking at him, but he isn't looking at her.

Here is Sue Peterson again. She has a car. She is parking her car in the parking lot at Kennedy Airport. She is meeting Jackie at the airport. Jackie is her friend. It's raining now and Sue doesn't have an umbrella.

5b

Say: **That's right.**
   OR
   That's wrong.

Jackie is on the plane.
   That's wrong.
She is at Kennedy Airport.
   That's right.

PICTURE ONE

1. The passengers are waiting for a plane.
2. Jackie is waiting for her suitcases.
3. They are coming.
4. She is wearing a coat.
5. Harry is wearing a coat and hat.

PICTURE TWO

1. Harry and Jackie aren't waiting now. They have their suitcases.
2. Harry has one suitcase.
3. Jackie has two suitcases.
4. Jackie is walking with Harry.
5. A porter is carrying her suitcases.

Now answer the questions.

PICTURE THREE

1. Who's this?
2. Where is he?
3. Is he carrying a suitcase?
4. What is he carrying?
5. What is he wearing?

PICTURE FOUR

1. And who's this?
2. Where is she?
3. Is she parking her car?
4. Who is she meeting?
5. Is it raining?

1 Look at the grammar: HAVE

He She	has doesn't have	a ticket. an umbrella. suitcases.
They	have don't have	

2 Say these sentences.

He **has** a coat. He **doesn't have** a hat.

She **has** a book. She **doesn't have** a newspaper.

They **have** suitcases. They **don't have** a ticket.

3 Look at the things in the picture. You can see ten things.

You can see:

1. a box of cigars
2. a pair of jeans
3. a bottle of scotch
4. a bottle of perfume
5. a dress
6. a suit
7. a blouse
8. toothbrushes
9. a shirt
10. sweaters

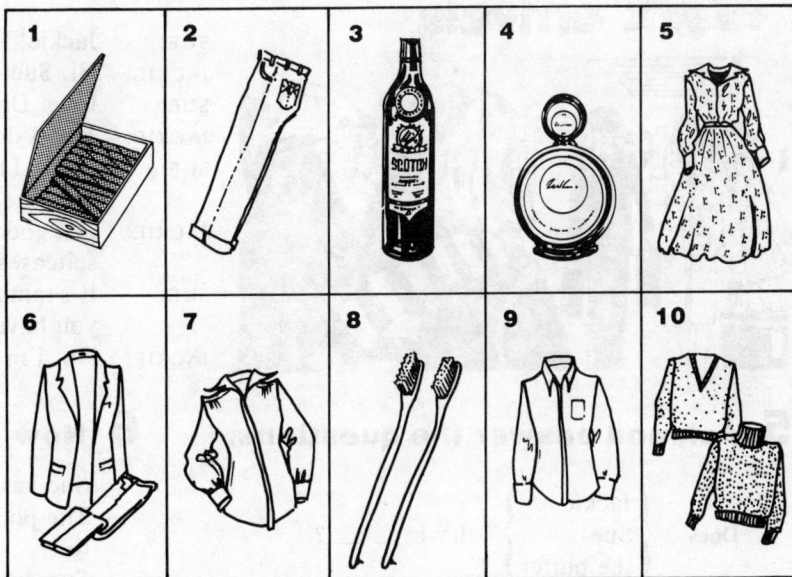

Now talk about Harry and Jackie.

He has .... in his suitcase.
She has .... in her suitcase.
They have .... in their suitcases.

18

5c

1 The policewoman is talking to Pat. 🎧

POLICEWOMAN:	Can I help you?
PAT:	No, thank you.
POLICEWOMAN:	What are you doing here? Are you waiting for a plane?
PAT:	Yes, I am.
POLICEWOMAN:	Well, do you have a ticket?
PAT:	No, I don't. I'm waiting for a friend. He's arriving on the plane from San Francisco.

2 Ask and answer the questions.

Does Pat have a ___? Yes, he **does**.
No, he **doesn't**.

Is he **waiting** for ___ ___? Yes, he **is**.
Is his friend **arriving** from ___ ___? No, he **isn't**.

3 Now talk about Pat.

He doesn't have a ___.
He's waiting for ___ ___.
His friend is arriving on the ___ from ___ ___.

4 Now listen to Sue and Jackie. 🎧

SUE:	Jackie! I'm over here! Hi!
JACKIE:	Hi, Sue. How are you?
SUE:	Fine. Do you have your suitcases?
JACKIE:	Yes, I do. A porter is bringing them.
SUE:	Good! I have my car. It's in the parking lot. I can take you to your hotel.
JACKIE:	Oh, good! Thanks! Porter, we can take the suitcases now.
SUE:	It's raining and I don't have an umbrella. Do you have one?
JACKIE:	No, I'm sorry. I don't have one either.

5 Ask and answer the questions.

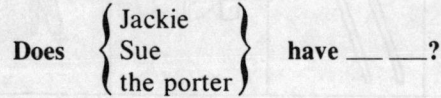

Does { Jackie / Sue / the porter } have ___ ___?

6 Now talk about the conversation.

Sue has ___ ___. It's ....
The porter is .... They're going to ....
Sue doesn't have ___ ___. Jackie doesn't have ___ either.

5d

1 Look at the grammar: HAVE

I We You They	have/don't have ....
He She	has/doesn't have ....

Do	I we you they	have .... ?
Does	he she	have .... ?

Yes, ___ do. No, ___ don't.
Yes, ___ does. No, ___ doesn't.

YOU SAY AND WRITE:

I **don't have** a car.
We **don't have** a car.
You **don't have** four suitcases.
They **don't have** raincoats.
She **doesn't have** two suitcases.
He **doesn't have** an umbrella.

YOU CAN ALSO WRITE:

I **do not have** a car.
We **do not have** a car.
You **do not have** four suitcases.
They **do not have** raincoats.
She **does not have** two suitcases.
He **does not have** an umbrella.

2 Look at Mike Brodsky again.
He is walking to a hotel near Grand Central Station.

Write questions and answers about Mike.

___ he ___ a car? No, ___ ___.

Does he have a car?
No, he doesn't.

1. ___ he ___ a bag? Yes, ___ ___.
2. ___ he ___ a suitcase? No, ___ ___.
3. ___ he ___ a hat? ___, ___ ___.
4. ___ he ___ an umbrella? ___, ___ ___.
5. ___ he ___ a guitar? ___, ___ ___.

3 What about you?

Do you have these things?

Example: a car

      I have a car.
OR **I don't have a car.**

1. a ticket to New York
2. a friend in New York
3. a friend in San Francisco
4. a raincoat
5. an umbrella
6. a dress
7. a suit
8. a shirt
9. a blouse
10. a guitar

4 Ask people in your class:

Do you **have** a ___?

Yes, I **do.**
No, I **don't.**

1. a ticket to New York
2. a friend in ___
3. a car
4. a guitar
5. ....
6. ....

5e

1 LISTEN

You can see two hotels in these pictures. One of them is near Central Park, a big park in New York. The other is near Grand Central Station.

The hotel on the left is the Park Hotel. It is big. It has five hundred rooms. The hotel on the right is the Lexington Hotel. It is small. It has twenty rooms.

The Lexington Hotel is between a bar and a garage.

A room at the Park Hotel is $65.00 a night. A room at the Lexington Hotel is $15.00 a night. The Park Hotel is very nice, but it is expensive. The Lexington Hotel is cheap.

Which hotel is Jackie going to? Is she going to the Park Hotel or to the Lexington Hotel? Which hotel is Mike going to?

2 Ask and answer the questions.

1. **Does** {the Park Hotel / the Lexington Hotel} **have** ___ rooms?
2. **Is** ___ {big? / small?}
3. **Is** ___ **going** to ___ ___ ___?
4. **How much is** a room at ___ ___ ___?
5. **Is** ___ ___ ___ {cheap? / expensive?}

3 Open Dialog

You are asking Jackie questions. What are they?

1. YOU: _____?
   JACKIE: Oh, I'm going to the Park Hotel.
2. YOU: _____?
   JACKIE: Yes, it is. It has five hundred rooms.
3. YOU: _____?
   JACKIE: $65.00 a night.
4. YOU: _____?
   JACKIE: It's on Fifth Avenue, near Central Park.

5f

1 This is Lucky. Lucky and Harry are partners. Lucky is meeting Harry at the airport. 🎧 LISTEN

LUCKY: How many suitcases do you have?
HARRY: Just one. This small one.
LUCKY: Can I help you?
HARRY: Yeah, here.
LUCKY: Hey, man, this suitcase is heavy! What do you have in it?
HARRY: Just clothes.
LUCKY: Just clothes?
HARRY: Yeah, two suits, three shirts, a pair of shoes . . . oh, and I have two boxes of cigars and four bottles of scotch . . . and my gun.

2 Answer the questions.

1. How many suitcases does Harry have?
2. Is it big or small?
3. Does he have just clothes in it?
4. How many boxes of cigars does he have?
5. How many bottles of scotch does he have?
6. What clothes does he have in his suitcase?

3 Say these numbers.

70 Seventy   **76** Seventy-six   **80** Eighty   **87** Eighty-seven   **90** Ninety

98 Ninety-eight   **100** One hundred   **109** One hundred and nine   **150** One hundred and fifty

4 Open Dialog

The porter is asking Jackie questions.

PORTER: __ __ suitcases __ __ __?
JACKIE: Just two.
PORTER: These suitcases are heavy! What __ __ __ in them?
JACKIE: Well, I have clothes in this one and books in that one.
PORTER: __ __ __ an umbrella? It's raining.
JACKIE: No, I don't.

22

UNIT 6 — A Room for the Night

6a

1

This is a room at the Lexington Hotel in New York.
It is a single. A single is a room for one person.
There is only one bed in this room.
There is a chair in the room too. It is next to the window. The room does not have a bathroom, but there is a sink next to the door.

2

And this is a room at the Park Hotel in New York.
It is a double. A double is a room for two people. There are two beds in this room.
There are two chairs in the room too. The room has a bathroom. There is a sink, a shower and a toilet in the bathroom.

3

Mike Brodsky is at the Lexington Hotel.

MIKE: Do you have a room?
CLERK: A single or a double?
MIKE: A single, please.
CLERK: Yeah, I have a single. Fifteen dollars a night. Can you pay now?
MIKE: Fifteen dollars? Sure.
CLERK: Okay. Sign here, please.

4

Jackie is at the Park Hotel.

CLERK: Good evening.
JACKIE: Good evening. My name is Hunter. I have a reservation.
CLERK: Oh, yes, Miss Hunter. Room four-oh-four. It's a double.
JACKIE: A double?
CLERK: Yes. But you can have it for the price of a single. Is that all right?
JACKIE: Yes, of course.

6b

PICTURE ONE

1. Where is this room?
2. How many beds can you see?
3. Is this room a single?
4. What is a single?
5. What can you see in the room?
6. *Ask and answer the questions:*
   Is the ___ next to the ___?

PICTURE TWO

1. Is this a room at the Lexington Hotel?
2. What can you see in it?
3. Is this a single or a double?
4. What is a double?
5. *Ask and answer:*
   Does the room have ___ ___?

PICTURE THREE

1. Where is Mike now?
2. Is his room a single or a double?
3. How much is it?
4. Is Mike paying now?

PICTURE FOUR:

1. Where is Jackie?
2. Is she paying too?
3. What is her room number?
4. Is it a single too?
5. Can she have it for the price of a single?

1 Look at the grammar: THERE IS/THERE ARE

There	is ('s)	only one bed a chair	here. in this room.
	are	two beds three chairs	there.

2 Write is ('s) or are.

There ___ one bed in his room.

There *is ('s)* one bed in his room.

There ___ two beds in her room.

There *are* two beds in her room.

1. There ___ one window in his room.
2. There ___ two windows in her room.
3. There ___ two chairs in her room too.
4. But in his room there ___ only one chair.
5. There ___ twenty rooms in the Lexington Hotel.
6. And in the Park Hotel there ___ five hundred rooms.

3 This isn't a hotel room. It's a classroom. What can you see in it? Ask and answer the questions.

How many	windows students teachers doors	are there in this classroom?

4 Now talk about your classroom.

There { is ('s) / are } ___ ___ in my classroom.

6c

1 Jackie is talking to the clerk at the Park Hotel. LISTEN

2 Now Mike is talking to the clerk at the Lexington Hotel. LISTEN

CLERK: How long are you staying, Miss Hunter?
JACKIE: Excuse me?
CLERK: How long are you staying?
JACKIE: Oh! Three nights.
CLERK: Three nights. Thank you. Are those your suitcases?
JACKIE: Yes, they are.
CLERK: Porter! Those are Miss Hunter's suitcases. Please take them to Room 404.
JACKIE: Thank you.
CLERK: Thank *you*, Miss Hunter.
JACKIE: Oh. Where's the elevator?
CLERK: It's on the left. Just follow the porter.

CLERK: How long are you staying?
MIKE: What?
CLERK: How long are you staying? How many nights?
MIKE: Uh . . . one night. I'm staying one night.
CLERK: OK. Here's your key. Room 16.
MIKE: Where is it?
CLERK: Three floors up.
MIKE: Is there an elevator?
CLERK: No, there isn't.
MIKE: Oh. Where are the stairs?
CLERK: On the right.

3 Ask and answer the questions.

How long is ___ staying?

Does ___ have a porter?

Is there an elevator in ___ hotel?

4 Open Dialog

You are at a hotel in New York.

CLERK: What ___ ___ name, please?
YOU: ___ ___.
CLERK: How ___ are you ___?
YOU: Two ___.
CLERK: Thank you. ___ those your suitcases?
YOU: Yes, they ___.
CLERK: Porter! Those are ___ ___'s suitcases. Please ___ them to ___ room.
YOU: Where's the ___?
CLERK: ___ ___ the right.

6d

1 LISTEN

It is midnight. Jackie is in her hotel room. She is writing a letter.

Mike is in bed. He is reading a book. There is a light over his bed.

Jackie is talking to the hotel operator.
JACKIE: This is Room 404. Please call me at seven o'clock.

Now Mike is setting his alarm clock. He is setting it for seven o'clock.

It is seven in the morning now and Jackie's phone is ringing.
OPERATOR: Good morning, Miss Hunter. It's seven o'clock.

Mike's alarm clock is ringing. He is getting up now too. He is tired.

And now it is seven thirty. Jackie is in her hotel room. Room Service is bringing her breakfast.
WAITER: Here's your breakfast, miss. Orange juice, toast and coffee.
JACKIE: Thank you.
WAITER: You're welcome.

Mike is eating breakfast in a cheap coffee shop.
WAITRESS: Here! Two eggs with bacon, toast and coffee. OK?
MIKE: Thanks.
WAITRESS: Sure.

2 Look at the answers. What are the questions?

1. Midnight.
2. In her hotel room.
3. She is writing.
4. A letter.
5. He is in bed.
6. Yes, he is.
7. A book.
8. Over his bed.
9. She is talking to the hotel operator.
10. No, she isn't in the room!
11. No, he isn't.
12. He is setting his alarm clock.
13. It is seven o'clock now.
14. No, not seven o'clock in the evening. Seven o'clock in the morning.
15. No, his telephone isn't ringing. His alarm clock is.
16. He is getting up.
17. No, she isn't in a coffee shop. She's in her hotel room.
18. No, he isn't. He's eating in a cheap coffee shop.

26

6e

1 🎧

Jackie is standing at her window. What can she see?

This is Central Park. It is a big park in New York. Jackie can see Central Park from her window. Look at the trees and the lake. She can see them too. She can also see the buses and the cars on Fifth Avenue. There's a policeman on a horse. She can see him too.

What can Mike see from his window? Can he see Central Park? Can he see trees, buses or cars?

2 Ask and answer the questions.

Can Jackie see ....?
Yes, she **can**./No, she **can't**.

Can Mike see ....?
Yes, he **can**./No, he **can't**.

3 Look at the letter and the postcard.

The letter is from Jackie to her father.
He is in San Francisco, California.
The postcard is from Mike Brodsky to his mother. She is in Newton, Massachusetts.
Newton is near Boston.
Can you see the stamp on Jackie's letter?
Is there a stamp on Mike's postcard?

Dear Mom,
New York is very expensive, but I have a cheap room at a small hotel. This is a picture of the United Nations. It's near my hotel.
Love,
Mike

POSTCARD

Mrs. Doris Brodsky
61 Green Street
Newton, MA 02158

Mr. M. Hunter
17 Laguna Street
San Francisco, CA
94114

4 Now answer the questions.

1. Who is the letter from?
2. Who is it to?
3. Where is Jackie's father?
4. Who is the postcard to?
5. Where is she?
6. Where is Newton?
7. Who is the postcard from?
8. Where is he now?

6f

1 LISTEN

It is nine o'clock in the morning now.
Jackie is at the hotel.

CLERK: Good morning, Miss Hunter.
JACKIE: Good morning. Can I buy stamps here?
CLERK: Certainly. For a letter or a postcard?
JACKIE: For a letter.
CLERK: Here you are. That's eighteen cents.
JACKIE: Thank you. Oh! Where's the mailbox?
CLERK: Over there near the elevators.
JACKIE: Thank you very much.
CLERK: You're welcome.

2 LISTEN

There's a post office two blocks from Mike's hotel. Mike can't buy stamps at his hotel, but he can buy stamps at the post office. And this is the post office.

MIKE: How much is a stamp for a postcard?
CLERK: Twelve cents.
MIKE: Can I have one, please?
CLERK: Here you are.
MIKE: Thank you.

3 Answer the questions.

1. What is Jackie buying?
2. What is Mike buying?
3. Where is he buying it?
4. Where is she buying it?
5. How much is her stamp?
6. How much is his stamp?

4 This is Jackie's letter to her father. Complete the letter.

Thursday
September 1

Dear Dad,
I ___ staying at the Park Hotel in New York. It ___ very nice.
I ___ a big room and I ___ see Central Park ___ my window.
I ___ tired and I'm going to bed in a minute.
Love,
Jackie

5 Open Dialog

You are staying at a very small hotel in New York. You can't buy stamps at this hotel.

YOU: ___ I ___ a stamp here?
CLERK: No, I'm sorry. We ___ have stamps here.
YOU: Oh. Where ___ I ___ one?
CLERK: There's a ___ ___ near the hotel.
YOU: ___ is it?
CLERK: Two blocks from here.
YOU: ___ you.

You are at the post office now.

YOU: ___ much ___ a stamp for a ___?
CLERK: ___ cents.
YOU: ___ I ___ one, please?
CLERK: Here ___ ___.
YOU: Thank ___.

READING AND WRITING FOLLOW-UP: Units 1–6

1 This is an announcement.

American Airlines announces the departure of Flight 16 to Dallas. This flight is leaving from Gate Twelve. This is the American nine thirty flight to Dallas.

Write an announcement for the second flight. (This is an Eastern Airlines flight.)

Now answer these questions about the third flight.

1. What time is Flight 72?
2. Where is Flight 72 going?
3. What gate is it leaving from?

You can see two other flights (National and United Airlines). Ask and answer questions about them.

2 This is Jackie's family.

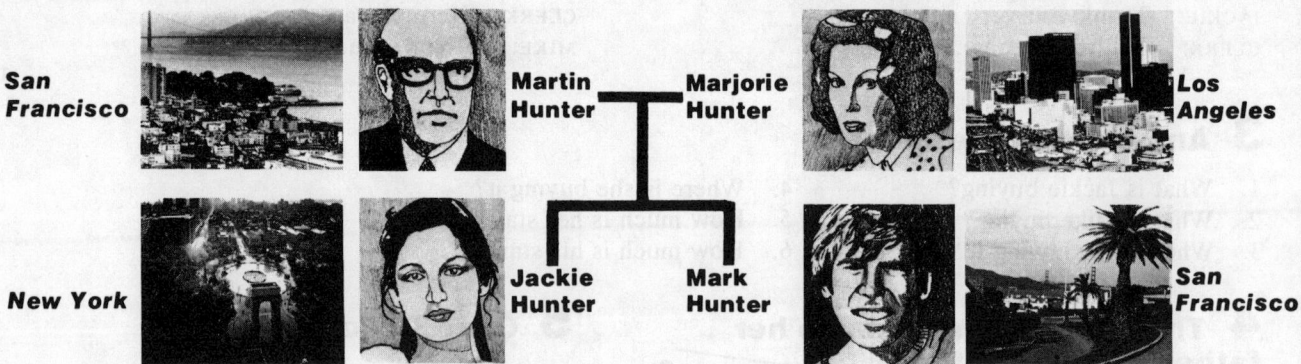

Martin Hunter is Jackie's father. He lives in San Francisco. Marjorie Hunter is Jackie's mother. She lives in Los Angeles. Jackie's parents are divorced. They have two children, Jackie and Mark.
Mark is Jackie's brother. She doesn't have a sister. Jackie lives in New York. She's single. She's not married.

Write about Mark Hunter.

Jackie ___ Mark's ___.
He doesn't have ___ ___.
Mark ___ ___ San Francisco.
He's not married.
He's ___.

3 Write about Mike's hotel.

```
◆◆◆◆◆◆◆◆◆◆◆◆◆◆◆◆◆◆◆◆◆◆◆◆
        LEXINGTON HOTEL
   ◆◆◆◆◆◆◆◆◆◆◆◆◆◆◆◆◆◆◆
  Lexington Avenue near 42nd Street
   ◆◆◆◆◆◆◆◆◆◆◆◆◆◆◆◆◆◆◆
  Small Hotel   20 Rooms   Cheap Rates

      Single without bath $15.00
      Double without bath $20.00

     ★Near Grand Central Station★
      ★ Coffee Shop on the Corner ★
◆◆◆◆◆◆◆◆◆◆◆◆◆◆◆◆◆◆◆◆◆◆◆◆
```

Mike is staying at the Lexington Hotel.

The Lexington Hotel ___ a hotel ___ Lexington Avenue ___ 42nd Street. A ___ room costs ___ and a ___ room ___ $20.00.
There isn't a restaurant in the Lexington Hotel, but ___ is a coffee shop ___ the corner.
Mike ___ a ___ room at the Lexington Hotel. ___ room costs ___. It ___ have a bathroom.

4 Read about Jackie's hotel.

The Park Hotel is an expensive hotel in New York City. It is on Central Park South near Fifth Avenue.

The Park Hotel has a coffee shop, two restaurants and a bar.

The Park Hotel has 500 rooms. The rooms are big and they have private bathrooms. A single room is $65.00, and a double room is $75.00 plus tax.

There are movies, theaters, restaurants and stores near the hotel and, of course, guests can walk in Central Park.

1. Is the Park Hotel cheap?
2. Where is the Park Hotel?
3. Does the hotel have a coffee shop?
4. How many restaurants does the hotel have?
5. How many rooms does the hotel have?
6. Do the rooms have private bathrooms?
7. How much is a single room? And a double?
8. Are there theaters near the hotel?

5 You are staying in Jackie's hotel for two nights. You have a double room. Write your hotel bill. How much is it?

The Park Hotel
1061 Fifth Avenue
New York, New York 10022

Name: JACQUELINE HUNTER
Address: 17 LAGUNA ST.
SAN FRANCISCO, CA 94113
Room: 404

Date		
9/1	ROOM	$ 65.00
	RESTAURANT	10.50
	BAR	4.25
9/2	ROOM	65.00
	RESTAURANT	11.95
9/3	ROOM	65.00
	RESTAURANT	19.10
	BAR	2.75

Total Hotel   243.55
Tax 8%   19.48
TOTAL $263.03

This is Jackie's hotel bill. How much is it?

This is Jackie's check.

JACQUELINE HUNTER   592
17 LAGUNA STREET
SAN FRANCISCO, CA 94113   Sept. 4   19 81

Pay to the
Order of   The Park Hotel $ 263.03
Two hundred sixty-three and 03/100 ——— Dollars

Center Bank
Union Square
San Francisco CA 94114   Jacqueline Hunter

Now write this check for your hotel bill.

The Park Hotel
1061 Fifth Avenue
New York, New York 10022

Name _____
Address _____   Room _____
_____
_____

Total Hotel
Tax 8%
TOTAL

_____ 19 ___

Pay to the
Order of _____ $ _____
_____ Dollars

Center Bank
Union Square
San Francisco CA 94114

UNIT 7 — A Job in Greenwich Village

7a

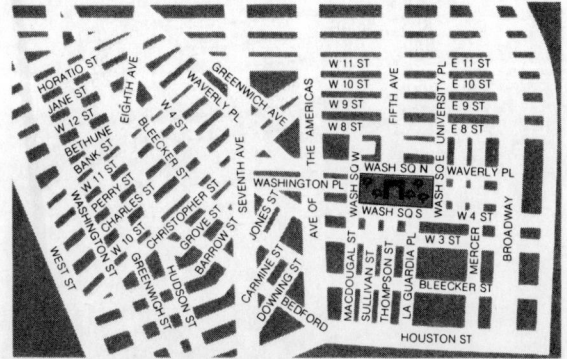

This is Greenwich Village. Greenwich Village is a part of New York.
There is a park in Greenwich Village. It is called Washington Square Park. Can you see it on the map?

And this is Eighth Street. Look at the people, the cars and the stores.
Can you see that big store? It is a supermarket. You can buy food there—meat, vegetables, fruit, bread and things like that.

There is a movie theater on Eighth Street. You can see movies there. What is playing today? Can you see it? *Texas Cowboy* is playing. It is a western. There is a bar next to the movie theater. The name of the bar is Shakespeare's. You can have a drink there. You can eat there too.

And this is a travel agency in Greenwich Village. You can buy tickets and you can get travel information here.

7b

1 The American Language Center is a school. You can learn English there. Bill Rivera is a teacher at the Center. He is teaching now. 🎧 LISTEN

PICTURE ONE

1. What can you see in picture one?
2. Is Greenwich Village a part of New York?
3. What is there in Greenwich Village?

PICTURE TWO

1. What can you see in this picture?
2. What is that big store?
3. What can you buy there?

PICTURE THREE

1. Where is this movie theater?
2. What is playing today?
3. What is *Texas Cowboy*?

PICTURE FOUR

1. And what is this in picture four?
2. What can you buy there?
3. And what can you get?

BILL: Look at this man and this woman. His name is Wonderman and her name is Wonderwoman. He can fly and she can fly too. He's very strong! He can lift a house. She's very strong too. She can't lift a house, but she can lift a car! And she can speak ten foreign languages too!

Wonderman can't speak any foreign languages. He can speak English. That's all.

2 Ask and answer the questions.

Can	Wonderman Wonderwoman	fly? lift a ___? speak ___?	Yes,	he she	can.
			No,	he she	can't.

3 Ask people in your class:

Can you ....? Yes, I can.
No, I can't.

32

7c

1 What are the people doing in these pictures? Can you do these things? 🎧 LISTEN

1. Harry is driving. Can you drive too?
2. Jackie is dancing. She can dance very well. What about you?
3. Mike is cooking, but he can't cook very well. Can you cook?
4. Bill is playing tennis. He can play tennis very well. Can you play tennis?
5. Mike is playing the guitar. What about you? Can you play the guitar too? Can you play the guitar very well?
6. Bill is swimming. But look at him! He can't swim very well. What about you?

2 Look at the grammar: CAN

I You He She We They	can	swim. dance. cook. drive.

Can	you he she they	swim? dance? cook? drive?

3 Now ask people in your class:

Can you ___?   Yes, I can.
             Yes, I can, but not very well.
             No, I can't.

7d

1 It is Friday, September 2 (September second). Marie Williams is the manager of a travel agency in Greenwich Village. She is talking to Carol Lee.

MARIE: Can you type, Carol?
CAROL: Yes, I can.
MARIE: How many words a minute?
CAROL: Eighty.
MARIE: Hmmm. And can you speak any foreign languages?
CAROL: Yes, I can. I speak Spanish and, of course, I speak Chinese.
MARIE: Really? That's very good! What about French?
CAROL: No, I can't speak French. But I can speak Italian. But not very well.
MARIE: Hmmm. Can you start next week?
CAROL: Next week?
MARIE: Yes. On Monday.
CAROL: You mean, I have the job?
MARIE: Yes, that's right. You have the job!

2 Ask and answer the questions.

Can Carol ....?
How many ___ can she ___?

3 Ask people in your class:

Can you ....?
How many ___ can you ___?

4 Now talk and write about Carol.

1. She ___ ___ eighty words a minute.
2. She ___ ___ Spanish and Chinese.
3. She ___ ___ French, but she ___ ___ Italian.

5 What about you?

Can you speak any foreign languages? Can you type? How many words a minute? Can you dance? Can you drive? Can you swim or play tennis? What can you do?

7e

1 🎧

This is a cheap apartment in Greenwich Village. There is one room and a bathroom in the apartment. There is a bed in the room and there are three chairs and a table too. Can you see them?

There is a small stove and a refrigerator in the room. Can you see them too?

Mike Brodsky is looking for an apartment like this.

2 🎧

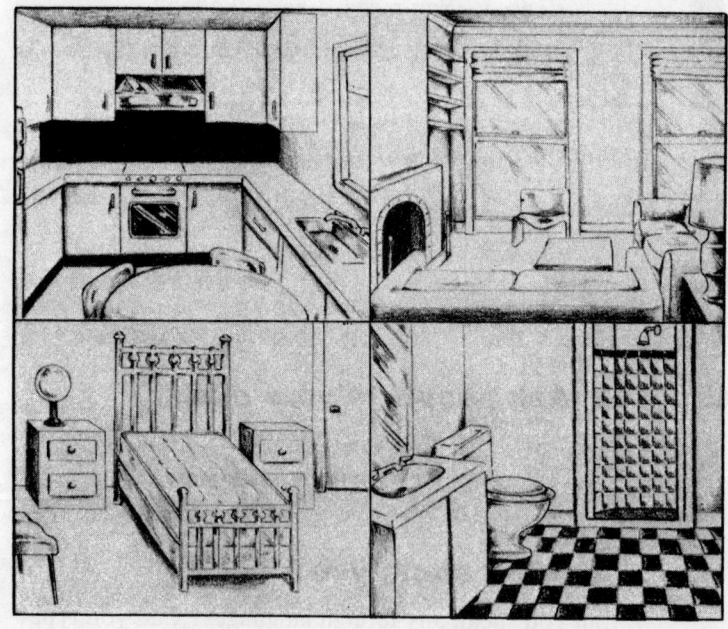

This is an expensive apartment in Greenwich Village. There are three rooms in this apartment. One room is the kitchen. There is a stove and a refrigerator in the kitchen. One room is the living room. One room is the bedroom. Which room is the kitchen? Which room is the living room? And which room is the bedroom?
There are two windows in the living room. Can you see them? There is a toilet and a shower in the bathroom. Can you see them too?
Jackie Hunter is looking for an apartment like this.

3 Ask and answer the questions.

    Is there a ___ in the ___?   How many ___ are there in the ___?   Where is the ___?

4 Now talk about your room or apartment or house.

    There is/are ___ in my ___.   I have/I don't have ___ in my ___.

35

7f

1 Mike Brodsky is calling about the cheap apartment. He is talking to the owner, Mrs. Jason. LISTEN

MRS. JASON: Hello?
MIKE: Hello. I'm calling about the apartment.
MRS. JASON: Oh, yes.
MIKE: Can you tell me about it, please?
MRS. JASON: Yes, it's a one-room apartment. There's a bed in it, of course. And there's a table and...
MIKE: And where is it? What's the address, I mean?
MRS. JASON: 19 Sullivan Street. It's near Washington Square.
MIKE: Uh-huh. And how much is the rent, please?
MRS. JASON: The rent? Two hundred dollars a month.
MIKE: Can I see the apartment, please?
MRS. JASON: Yes, of course. Can you come now?
MIKE: Yes. In ten or fifteen minutes. Is that all right?
MRS. JASON: Yes, that's all right.
MIKE: Goodbye.
MRS. JASON: Oh! Wait! What's your name?
MIKE: Mike Brodsky.
MRS. JASON: Can you spell it, please?
MIKE: B-R-O-D-S-K-Y.
MRS. JASON: Thank you, Mr. Brodsky. See you in ten or fifteen minutes.

2 Open Dialog

And now Jackie is calling about the expensive apartment. She is talking to the owner, Mr. Young. What is she saying?

MR. YOUNG: Hello?
JACKIE: ___ ___ ___ the apartment. ___ ___ tell ___ ___ ___?
MR. YOUNG: Yes, of course. What can I tell you about it?
JACKIE: Well, ___ many rooms ___ there in ___ apartment?
MR. YOUNG: There are three rooms: a bedroom, a living room and a kitchen. And of course, there's a bathroom.
JACKIE: ___ ___ ___?
MR. YOUNG: It's in Greenwich Village, near Washington Square.
JACKIE: ___ ___ ___?
MR. YOUNG: Two Fifth Avenue.
JACKIE: ___ ___ ___ ___ ___?
MR. YOUNG: Six hundred dollars a month.
JACKIE: ___ ___ ___ ___ ___, please?
MR. YOUNG: Yes, of course. Can you come now?
JACKIE: Yes. In thirty ___ forty minutes. ___ ___ all right?
MR. YOUNG: Yes, that's all right.
JACKIE: Goodbye.
MR. YOUNG: Bye.

3 Write about the apartment.

apartment/near Washington Square

The apartment is near Washington Square.

1. three rooms and a bathroom/the apartment
2. rent/$600 a month
3. two windows/living room
4. a table/kitchen
5. address/Two Fifth Avenue

UNIT 8
Monday Morning

8a

It is Monday morning, October 6 (sixth).
It is seven in the morning. The sun is shining.
Can you see that big apartment building? It is near Washington Square Park.
Jackie Hunter lives there now. She lives in an apartment near Washington Square.
Her address is Two Fifth Avenue, New York, New York 10011.

Marie Williams is getting up. The man in bed is her husband. His name is Tom Williams. Marie and Tom are married. They live in the same apartment building. Their address is Two Fifth Avenue too.

MARIE: Come on, Tom. Get up. It's seven o'clock. The sun's shining.
TOM: Oh . . . no! Turn on the radio, please.

What's on the radio this morning?
Andrea Steele is on. She is a disc jockey. Her program is starting.

ANDREA: Good morning. This is Andrea Steele with your favorite music. And here's our first record this morning. It's called "Hello, Sun."

But Jackie can't hear Andrea. She isn't listening to her. She is running in Washington Square Park. A man is watching Jackie. He can see her, but she can't see him. He is standing behind a tree.

8b

1 Say That's right. or That's wrong.

Jackie and Tom Williams are married.   That's wrong.
Marie and Tom Williams are married.   That's right.

PICTURE ONE

1. Is it September now?
2. What month is it?
3. What can you see in the first picture?
4. What is Jackie's address now?

1. Jackie lives near Washington Square Park.
2. Marie and Tom live near Washington Square Park too.
3. They live in a house.
4. They live in an apartment.
5. Jackie lives in a house.
6. Andrea Steele is listening to Jackie.
7. Jackie is listening to her.
8. Marie and Tom are listening to her.
9. Jackie is running and a man is watching her.

2 Look at the grammar: Simple Present

I We You They	live	in New York. in the United States. in a house. in an apartment.
He She	lives	

PICTURE TWO

1. Who can you see in the second picture?
2. *Talk about Marie and Tom.*
   They ___ married.
   They ___ in an apartment.

3 Talk and write about Bill, Sue and Mike.

1. He ___ in an apartment.
2. ___ address ___ 99 Bank Street, New York, New York 10014.

PICTURE THREE

1. Who can you see in the third picture?
2. Who is Andrea Steele?
3. What is the first record this morning?

3. She ___ ___ an apartment too.
4. ___ address ___ 21 Greenwich Avenue, New York, New York 10014.

5. ___ ___ ___ an apartment.
6. ___ address ___ 19 Sullivan Street, New York, New York 10014.

PICTURE FOUR

1. What can you see in the fourth picture?
2. *Talk about Jackie:*
   She ___ running.
   She ___ in an apartment.
3. *Talk about the man.*
   Where is he?
   What is he doing?

4 What about you?

1. ___ ___ ___ a house/an apartment.
2. ___ address ___ ....

8c

1 It is eight fifteen now. Marie and Tom Williams are leaving their apartment. The boy with them is Bobby, their son. And that man is a mailman. 🎧 LISTEN

MAILMAN: Excuse me. Do you live here?
MARIE: Yes, we do. We live on the third floor.
MAILMAN: Oh. Does Jackie Hunter live here too?
MARIE: Who? Jackie Hunter? Do you know that name, Tom?
TOM: Jackie Hunter? No, I don't. I'm sorry.
BOBBY: I know her!
TOM: Do you? Does she live here?
BOBBY: Yes, she does. She's from California! She lives under us. She lives in the apartment on the second floor!
MAILMAN: Oh, thanks! I have a letter for her, but her name isn't on the mailbox.

2 Look at these questions and answers.

Does	Jackie Hunter / Mike Brodsky	live here?	Yes,	she	does.
			No,	he	doesn't.

Now can you answer the questions?

1. Does Marie Williams live in an apartment?
2. Does Tom live in an apartment too?
3. Does Bobby live there?
4. Does Jackie live in an apartment too?
5. Does Bobby know her name?
6. Does Marie know her?
7. Does Bobby know her?
8. Does the mailman know her?
9. Does Jackie live on the third floor?
10. Does Bobby live on the second floor?

3 Now look at these questions and answers.

Do	you	live here? / know Jackie Hunter?	Yes, I do.
			No, I don't.

4 What about you?

1. Do you live near Washington Square Park?
2. Do you live in Greenwich Village?
3. Do you live in New York?
4. Do you live in a city?
5. Do you live near a city?
6. Do you live in a house?
7. Do you live in an apartment?
8. Do you live near a park?

5 Open Dialogs

You are talking to Mike Brodsky.
Mike lives in an apartment in Greenwich Village.

What are your questions?
What are his answers?

YOU: ___ you ___ ___ Greenwich Village?
MIKE: ___, ___ ___.
YOU: ___, ___ ___ ___ house?
MIKE: ___, ___ ___. I ___ ___ ___ apartment.

And now Harry is talking to Lucky.
He's asking questions about Jackie Hunter.

What are Harry's questions?
What are Lucky's answers?

HARRY: ___ she ___ in Greenwich Village?
LUCKY: Yes, ___ ___.
HARRY: ___ ___ ___ ___ house?
LUCKY: No, ___ ___. She ___ ___ ___ apartment.

8d

1 Where do they work?

Marie Williams works in a travel agency.
She is the manager. Carol Lee works there too.
Marie is Carol's boss.

Tom Williams works in a factory.
He is an engineer.

And now listen to Sue Peterson and Bill Rivera.

SUE: I work in an office. I'm not a secretary. I'm a newspaper reporter. I work for the *Village News*. It's a small newspaper in Greenwich Village.

BILL: And me? I'm a teacher. I work in Greenwich Village too. I teach English at the American Language Center.

2 Ask and answer the questions.

Does	Marie Carol Tom Bill Sue	work	in a factory? in a travel agency? in an office?
		teach	English?

3 Ask people in your class:

Do you	work live	in a ___? in an ___?

8e

1

And this is Carol Lee again.
What about her?
Carol is not married. She lives in a house in Rye.
Rye is a town near New York City.
Carol lives with her father. Her mother is dead.

2

Carol is going to work now. She has a new job at a travel agency in New York City. It is her first day today.

CAROL:	Dad! I'm going to work now.
MR. LEE:	Oh! Goodbye, Carol.
CAROL:	See you tonight.
MR. LEE:	Yes, bye!

3

Carol is waiting for her train now. She is at Rye Station. She can see a friend. Her friend works in New York City too.

CAROL:	Hello, Donna! How are you?
DONNA:	Fine, thanks. And you?
CAROL:	I'm fine, thanks. Are you going to work?
DONNA:	Yes, I am. Where are you going?
CAROL:	I'm going to work too. I have a new job in Greenwich Village.

4

And now Carol is at the travel agency. Marie Williams is her boss. The man and the other woman work there too.

MARIE:	Carol, this is Betty Jensen. Betty, this is Carol Lee.
CAROL:	Nice to meet you, Betty.
BETTY:	Nice to meet you too.
MARIE:	And this is Luis Martinez.
LUIS:	Hello.
CAROL:	Hi.

8f

1 Look at the grammar: Simple Present

I / You / They / We	live work	in ___.

He / She	lives works	in ___.

Do	you they	live work	in ___?

Yes,	I we they	do.
No,		don't.

Does	he she	live work	in ___?

Yes,	he she	does.
No,		doesn't.

PICTURE ONE

1. ___ Carol live in New York City?
   No, ___ ___.
2. ___ she ___ in Rye?
   Yes, ___ ___.

PICTURE TWO

1. ___ Carol going to work now?
   ___, ___ ___.
2. Is her father ___ to work too?
   No, ___ ___.

PICTURE THREE

1. Where ___ Carol now?
   She ___ at ___.
2. ___ she see a friend?
   Yes, ___ ___.
3. ___ her friend ___ to work?
   Yes, she ___.
4. Does she ___ in New York City?
   Yes, ___ ___.

PICTURE FOUR

1. ___ Betty Jensen Carol's boss?
   No, ___ ___.
2. ___ Betty work at the travel agency?
   ___, ___ ___.
3. ___ Luis Martinez ___ there too?
   ___, ___ ___.

2 Open Dialog

Luis Martinez is talking to Carol Lee. It is one o'clock. They are having lunch.

LUIS: ___ you ___ in Greenwich Village, Carol?
CAROL: No, ___ ___ live in New York City. I ___ ___ Rye.
LUIS: Oh, ___ you married?
CAROL: No, ___ ___. But I ___ with a man.
LUIS: Oh, really?
CAROL: Yes, ___ ___ with ___ father.

3 Complete the letter from Jackie to her father.

October 4

___ Dad,
I ___ in Greenwich Village now. ___ have a very nice apartment here. I ___ see Washington Square Park ___ my window. I have ___ new friend in my apartment building. ___ name is Bobby Williams. I ___ ___ the second ___ and he ___ ___ the ___ floor. ___ is 10! His father ___ in a factory. ___ mother ___ in a travel agency.

UNIT 9
Watching Jackie

9a

This is Jackie Hunter again. You know this about her: She lives in Greenwich Village and she is from San Francisco.
But you don't know this about her: She is a student in New York and she goes to New York University Law School. Her father lives in San Francisco. He is president of a bank and he is very rich.

It is Friday, November 4 (fourth) now and it is seven o'clock in the morning. Jackie is getting up. She always gets up at seven o'clock in the morning. She always runs in Washington Square Park. She runs there every morning, seven days a week.

It is seven thirty now and Jackie is having breakfast. She is listening to Andrea Steele's radio program. It always starts at seven o'clock. Jackie always has breakfast at seven thirty and she always listens to her.

ANDREA: Hi, everybody. You're listening to Andrea Steele. It's seven thirty. Are you getting up?

Jackie starts school at nine. It is eight thirty now and she is leaving her apartment. She always leaves at eight thirty. Jackie finishes school at three o'clock.

ANDREA: Well, that's all for this morning. Bye!

9b

PICTURE ONE

What are the questions and answers?

1. Where ___ Jackie live?
2. ___ her father ___ in New York too?
3. Where ___ he live?
4. ___ he rich?
5. ___ Jackie go to New York University Law School?

PICTURE TWO

Answer the questions.

1. Is Jackie running now?
2. Is she getting up?
3. What time is it?
4. What time does she get up in the morning?
5. What about you? What time do you get up?

PICTURE THREE

Talk about Jackie.

1. She is ....
2. She always ....

Ask questions about Jackie.

3. Is Jackie ....?
4. Does she always ....?

PICTURE FOUR

Answer the questions.

1. Is she listening to the radio now?
2. Is she leaving her apartment?
3. Does she always leave the apartment at eight thirty?
4. What time does she start school?
5. What time does she finish school?

1 Say the verbs and then say the sentences.

lives   starts   finishes

1. Jackie **lives** in New York now.
2. She **starts** school at nine o'clock.
3. She **finishes** at three o'clock.

2 This is Mike Brodsky. Do you remember him?

LISTEN

MIKE: I live in a small apartment in Greenwich Village. I get up at eight or eight thirty. Sometimes I get up at nine.

I have breakfast at eight thirty or nine. And sometimes I don't have breakfast at all.

I'm a student. I don't go to New York University Law School. I go to Columbia University.

3 Talk and write about Jackie and Mike.

1. He lives in an ___ and she ....
2. She gets up at ___ and he ....
3. She ___ breakfast at ___ and he ....
4. She goes to .... and he ....

4 What about you?

1. I live ....
2. I get up at ....
3. I have breakfast at ....
4. I leave my apartment/house at ....
5. I start school/work at .... and I finish at ....

44

9c

1 Do you remember Harry Gilmore? He is talking to Lucky Jones. And they are talking about Jackie again. LISTEN

HARRY: All right, Lucky. You watch this girl every day. When does she leave her apartment in the morning?
LUCKY: She leaves at eight thirty.
HARRY: Every morning?
LUCKY: No. Not on Saturday or Sunday.
HARRY: Hmm. When does she have lunch?
LUCKY: Usually at one.
HARRY: Usually? Not always?
LUCKY: No. Sometimes she doesn't have lunch at all.
HARRY: Hmm. And where does she have lunch?
LUCKY: Sometimes in a coffee shop near the school. And sometimes in the school cafeteria.
HARRY: I see. Now, what does she do in the afternoon?
LUCKY: Well, she usually goes to the library. She gets home at five or five thirty. I think she usually has dinner at six thirty or seven.
HARRY: You *think*? Do you *know*?
LUCKY: No, I don't. But I know she often watches television in the evening and sometimes she goes to a bar.
HARRY: A bar? What bar?
LUCKY: Shakespeare's. It's on Eighth Street. She goes there with some friends.
HARRY: Some friends? Who?
LUCKY: I don't know their names.

2 Look at this question again.

When (What time) does Jackie leave her apartment?
She leaves **at eight thirty**.

Now answer these questions.

1. When does she have lunch?
2. Does she always have lunch at one?
3. Where does she go in the afternoon?
4. When does she get home?
5. When does she have dinner?
6. Does Lucky know this or does he think this?
7. When does she watch television?
8. Where does she go in the evening?

3 Ask people in your class:

When What time	do you	get up? have breakfast? go to work/school? have lunch/dinner? get home? go to bed?

4 What about you?

	always usually often (sometimes)		get up leave home ___ to school/ work ___ lunch ___ home ___ to bed	at ___.
I				
Sometimes		I		

45

9d

1 🎧 LISTEN

It is eight o'clock in the evening now. Jackie is sitting in her apartment. She often watches television in the evening. Sometimes she listens to records in the evening and sometimes she reads. Can you see the stereo and the records? There are some books in that bookcase.

What is she doing now?

Mike is sitting on the floor of his apartment. He never watches television. He doesn't have a television. He doesn't have a stereo either. But he often listens to the radio. Sometimes he reads books. There are some books on the table. Can you see them?

Mike isn't a very good student. Mike often plays his guitar at Shakespeare's. He sings too.

What is he doing now?

2 Look at these questions and answers.

Is Jackie **listening** to records now?
No, she **isn't.**

Does she sometimes **listen** to records in the evening?
Yes, she **does.**

3 Can you ask and answer these questions about Jackie?

1. ___ she sitting in her apartment?
   Yes, she ___.
2. ___ she listen to records in the evening?
   Yes, she ___.
3. Does she ___ television too?
   ___, she ___.
4. Is she ___ television now?
   Yes, she ___.

4 Now ask questions about Mike. What are the answers?

Does he .... in the evening?
Is he ___ing now?

5 Ask people in your class:

What do you do in the evening?

I	often never usually always (sometimes)	___ television. ___ to the movies. ___ to the radio. ___ to records. ___ books. ___ the guitar.
Sometimes	I	

9e

1
It is nine thirty and Jackie is at Shakespeare's with Bill and Sue. Bill and Sue are her friends. Mike is playing his guitar. He is finishing now. LISTEN

SUE: Hmm. Very good. He plays very well.
JACKIE: Yes, I think so too. What's his name?
SUE: I don't know. Bill, do you know him?
BILL: Yes, I do. His name's Mike Brodsky. He's a student. He often plays the guitar here.
JACKIE: Really? When?
BILL: Well, usually on Wednesdays and Fridays.
JACKIE: Oh.
SUE: He's coming over here now.
BILL: Hi, Mike!
MIKE: Hi, Bill. How are you?
BILL: Fine, thanks. Oh, Mike, this is Sue Peterson. And this is Jackie Hunter.
SUE: Nice to meet you, Mike.
MIKE: Nice to meet you too. And . . . I'm sorry . . . what's your name?
JACKIE: Jackie. Jackie Hunter.
MIKE: Nice to meet you. Do you come here often?
JACKIE: No, not very often. Sometimes on Saturdays.
MIKE: Oh, I don't play on Saturdays . . . . Cigarette?
JACKIE: No, thanks. I don't smoke.

2 Ask and answer the questions.

Does ___ know ___?
When does ....?
Does ___ think Mike plays well?

3 Talk about the conversation, like this:

.... knows ...., but .... doesn't know ....
.... often ....
.... comes to Shakespeare's on ....

4 Open Dialog

You are talking to Bill at Shakespeare's.
What are his questions? What are your answers?

BILL: ___ ___ name?
YOU: ___ ___.
BILL: Where ___ ___ from?
YOU: ___ ___ ___.
BILL: Oh! ___ is Jackie Hunter and Sue Peterson.
YOU: Nice ___ ___ ___.
BILL: ___ you ___ here often?
YOU: ___ ___ ___.

5 Say and write these sentences. Use her, him or them.

Bill knows Sue.
He knows her.

1. Jackie knows Bill.
2. Mike knows Bill.
3. Sue knows Jackie.
4. Jackie knows Sue and Bill.
5. Harry knows Jackie.
6. Jackie doesn't know Harry.

9f

1 Look at the grammar: Simple Present

He She	lives in New York. works in an office. watches television in the evening. goes to school in New York. plays the guitar.

I We They You	live in ___. work in ___. watch television in the evening too. go to school in ___. play the ___.

Do	I we they you	live in ___? work in ___? watch ___? go to ___?
Does	he she	play the ___?

Yes,	I we they you	do.	No,	I we they you	don't.
	he she	does.		he she	doesn't.

2 What is Bill saying?

I ___ in an apartment in New York. ___ address ___ 99 Bank Street. ___ ___ English at the American Language Center.

___ usually ___ breakfast ___ 8 in the morning. And ___ ___ lunch ___ 12 or 1 o'clock ___ ___ small restaurant ___ school.

___ ___ evening ___ often ___ television or ___ to records. ___ Wednesdays and Fridays ___ usually ___ to Shakespeare's. ___ Saturdays ___ often ___ to the movies ___ Sue Peterson.

3 Ask and answer these questions about Bill.

1. ___ he ___ English? Yes, ___ ___.
2. ___ he usually ___ breakfast at ___? ___, he ___.
3. When ___ he usually ___ lunch? At ___ ___ ___ ___.
4. Where ___ he usually ___ lunch? ___ ___ ___ ___.
5. ___ he often ___ television in the ___? Yes, ___ ___.

4 Now write about Bill.

He lives .... teaches ....
He often/usually ....
On Wednesdays and Fridays he ....
etc.

5 What about you?

I live/work in ....
___ go to ....
___ usually get up at ....
___ ___ breakfast at ....
I often/usually .... in the evening.

6 Bill is asking you questions. What are they? What are the answers?

1. Where ___ you live? I ___ ___ ___ ___.
2. ___ you work ___ a factory? ___, ___ ___.
3. ___ you ___ to Columbia University? ___, ___ ___.
4. When ___ you ___ up in the morning? I usually ___ ___ at ___ ___.
5. ___ time ___ have breakfast? ___ usually ___ at ___ ___.
6. ___ do you usually ___ ___ evening? I ....

READING AND WRITING FOLLOW-UP: Units 7–9

1 Look at the morning radio programs.

Ask and answer the questions.

1. What's on at seven o'clock?
2. What can you hear on this program?

Now ask and answer questions about the other programs.

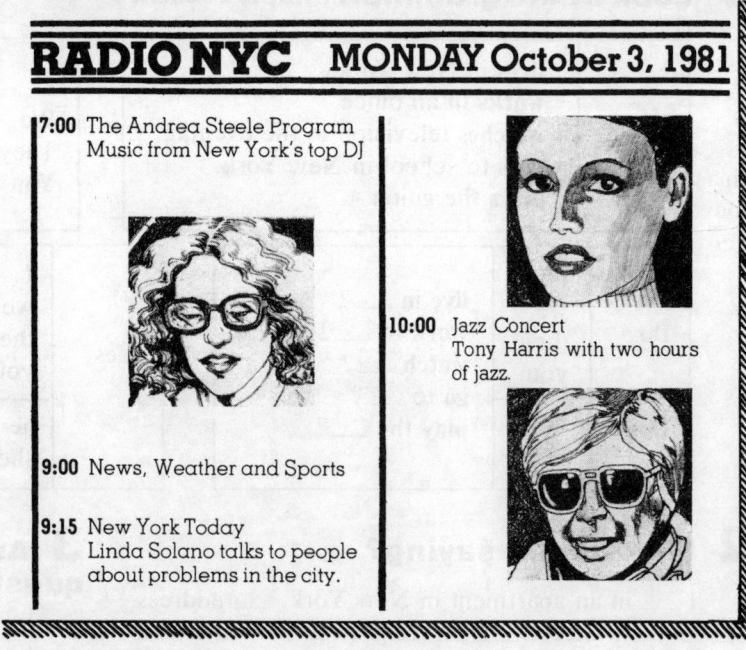

RADIO NYC   MONDAY October 3, 1981

7:00 The Andrea Steele Program
      Music from New York's top DJ

10:00 Jazz Concert
      Tony Harris with two hours of jazz.

9:00 News, Weather and Sports

9:15 New York Today
      Linda Solano talks to people about problems in the city.

2 Read about apartments and rooms for rent in New York.

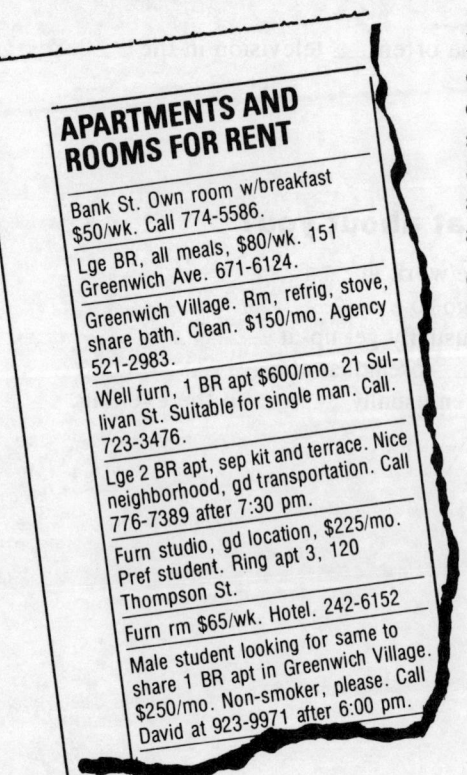

APARTMENTS AND ROOMS FOR RENT

Bank St. Own room w/breakfast $50/wk. Call 774-5586.

Lge BR, all meals, $80/wk. 151 Greenwich Ave. 671-6124.

Greenwich Village. Rm, refrig, stove, share bath. Clean. $150/mo. Agency 521-2983.

Well furn, 1 BR apt $600/mo. 21 Sullivan St. Suitable for single man. Call 723-3476.

Lge 2 BR apt, sep kit and terrace. Nice neighborhood, gd transportation. Call 776-7389 after 7:30 pm.

Furn studio, gd location, $225/mo. Pref student. Ring apt 3, 120 Thompson St.

Furn rm $65/wk. Hotel. 242-6152

Male student looking for same to share 1 BR apt in Greenwich Village. $250/mo. Non-smoker, please. Call David at 923-9971 after 6:00 pm.

Foreign students in New York usually live in apartments or dormitories. Sometimes students share their apartments or dormitory rooms. In other words, they live in them with other students. In a dormitory, you sometimes get meals too. Sometimes students can rent a room in another person's apartment or house. You can see advertisements for apartments and rooms in the newspapers.

Can you understand the ads here?

w/ = with	apt = apartment
BR = bedroom	mo = month
wk = week	sep = separate
rm = room	kit = kitchen
lge = large	gd = good
furn = furnished	pref = prefer or preferred

A student named Michiko lives in the room in the first ad.

Write about her.
Michiko ___ in a ___ on ___ ___.
She ___ $50 a ___ for this ___.

Look at the ad for the furnished one-bedroom apartment. A student named Carl lives in this apartment. What can you write about him?

3 Here is a registration form for the American Language Center. Complete it for Angela and Toshi.

Angela Risi is Italian. She's twenty-two. She lives at 34 Greenwich Avenue. She doesn't have a telephone. She wants to study at the Center for three months. She doesn't want to study English all the time. She wants to do other things too.

Toshi Ogawa is Japanese. He's thirty-five. He lives at 17 Sullivan Street. His telephone number is 485-2132. He can only study at the Center for three months. He wants to learn a lot of English in three months.

What about you?
I'm ___ (nationality).
I'm ___ (age).
I want to { ___ in the United States for ___ ___.
            ___ to the United States for ___ ___.

AMERICAN LANGUAGE CENTER

Complete and send to American Language Center, 450 Sixth Avenue, New York, N.Y. 10011

Last name _____ First name _____
Nationality _____ Age _____ Sex ☐ M
Address _____   ☐ F
_____ Telephone number _____

Please check (✓) the program you want
☐ Full-time (12 weeks, 25 hours/week) $300.00
☐ Part-time (12 weeks, 6 hours/week) $90.00

Enclosed is a check for _____

_____
(Signature)   (Date)

4 Bill Rivera teaches at the American Language Center. This is a letter from one of his students to a new pen pal.

You are Carlos' pen pal.

Write a letter to Carlos about yourself. Tell him about:
1. your school
2. where you are from
3. where you live
4. your family (how many brothers and sisters)

November 17

Dear Pen Pal,

    My name is Carlos Gomez. I'm from Caracas, Venezuela and I'm a student at the American Language Center. It's a language school in New York City. I like it here. The classes are small. There are four other students in my class. They are friendly and they come from different countries. One comes from Paris. There are two women from Japan. And there is a man from Egypt. I'm the fifth student.
    My teacher's name is Bill Rivera. I like him very much. He's a good teacher. We have three classes in the morning with him. We have two classes in the afternoon, but we have a different teacher.
    In Venezuela I work in a travel agency. American tourists often come to the agency. Usually they don't speak Spanish. And that is why I'm learning English now.
    I live with my family in Caracas in an apartment. My mother works in a bank and my father works in a factory. I have a brother and a sister. My brother is eighteen and my sister is twenty-two. My sister goes to the university. She's studying medicine. My brother doesn't like school. He has a job now in a garage. He's a mechanic there. He loves cars.
    Well, all this is about me. But what about you? Please write and tell me about yourself.

                      Sincerely,
                        Carlos
                        Carlos

UNIT 10
The Burglar

10a

1

It is Friday, December 9 (ninth).
It is exactly twelve noon.
Tom Williams works in a factory. He is having lunch in the factory cafeteria.
His wife, Marie, doesn't work in a factory.
She works in a travel agency.
She isn't having lunch. She is dictating a letter to her secretary.

2

Jackie Hunter goes to New York University Law School.
One of her teachers is giving a lecture. She is taking notes.
Mike Brodsky doesn't go to New York University Law School. He goes to Columbia University.
He is listening to a lecture now too.

3

Sue Peterson works for a newspaper.
She is writing an article now.
Bill Rivera doesn't work for a newspaper.
He teaches English.
He is teaching now. His class starts at 11:10 and ends at noon.

4

Bill lives in an apartment near school.
There is a man in his apartment now.
The man doesn't live in the apartment and Bill doesn't know him.
The man is a burglar and he is stealing things from Bill's apartment.

51

10b

1 These things are wrong. Answer like this:

Mike works in a factory.
> No, that's wrong. He doesn't work in a factory.

1. Tom works in a travel agency.
2. Marie works in a factory.
3. Jackie goes to Columbia University.
4. Mike goes to New York University Law School.
5. Sue Peterson teaches English.
6. Bill Rivera works for a newspaper.
7. The burglar lives in Bill's apartment.
8. Bill knows the burglar.

2 Do you remember Carol Lee?
Do you remember these things about her?

Carol lives in a house.
She lives in Rye.
Rye is a town near New York City.

Carol works in New York City.
She works in a travel agency in Greenwich Village.
Marie Williams is her boss.
Carol starts at nine every morning and finishes at five thirty.
She goes to work by train and she goes home by train too.

Ask and answer these questions.

Where ....?
Does ....?
Is ....?

3 Talk and write about Carol.

1. Carol doesn't ___ in a factory and she ___ teach English.
2. She doesn't ___ in an apartment and she ___ live in Greenwich Village.

PICTURES ONE, TWO AND THREE

Look at this question and this answer.

What is Tom doing now?
   He is having lunch.

Ask and answer the questions.

What is { Marie / Jackie / Mike / Sue / Bill } doing?

He / She is ___ing.

Now ask and answer these questions.

Does	Tom Marie Jackie Sue Mike Bill	work in ___? teach ___? go to ___? work for ___?

Yes, ___ does.
No, ___ doesn't.

PICTURE FOUR

1. Who is this man?
2. Where is he?
3. What is he doing?
4. Does he live in the apartment?
5. Can Bill see him?
6. Does Bill know him?

52

10c

1 But what about the burglar in Bill Rivera's apartment? LISTEN

A man can see him. The man is Mr. Benson and he lives across the street. He lives in an apartment on the fourth floor. Bill lives in an apartment on the fourth floor too. Mr. Benson is calling the police.

MR. BENSON: There's a burglar in the apartment.
POLICEMAN: In your apartment?
MR. BENSON: No! There isn't a burglar in my apartment. He's in Mr. Rivera's apartment. I can see him.
POLICEMAN: Who? Mr. Rivera?
MR. BENSON: No, you don't understand! I can't see Mr. Rivera, but I can see a man in Mr. Rivera's apartment. I can see him through the window.
POLICEMAN: And the man isn't Mr. Rivera?
MR. BENSON: No, he isn't.
POLICEMAN: Are you sure?
MR. BENSON: Yes, of course I am! I know Mr. Rivera! But I don't know the man in his apartment! He's stealing things! Please hurry!

2 Answer the questions.

1. Where does Mr. Benson live?
2. What can he see?
3. Who is he calling?
4. Does Mr. Benson know the man in Bill's apartment?
5. Who is the man?
6. What is he doing?

3 These things are wrong. Answer like this:

Mr. Benson is a burglar.
No! He isn't a burglar.
He knows the burglar.
No! He doesn't know the burglar.

1. Mr. Benson lives in Bill's apartment.
2. He can see Bill.
3. He is calling Bill.
4. He knows the man in Bill's apartment.
5. The policeman understands.
6. Mr. Benson is a policeman.
7. The policeman knows the burglar.
8. The burglar can hear Mr. Benson.
9. The burglar is a policeman.
10. The burglar is stealing things from Mr. Benson's apartment.

4 Talk and write about Mr. Benson.

1. Mr. Benson lives ....
2. He can see a ___ in ....
3. He is calling ___ ___ .
4. He knows ...., but he doesn't know ....

10d

1
It is two o'clock in the afternoon now and the police have the burglar. They are asking him questions. 🎧

POLICEMAN:	All right, what's your name?
FRANK:	Frank.
POLICEWOMAN:	Frank what? What's your last name?
FRANK:	Mitchum.
POLICEMAN:	How do you spell it?
FRANK:	F-R-A-...
POLICEMAN:	No! Not your first name! Spell your last name!
FRANK:	M-I-T-C-H-U-M.
POLICEWOMAN:	Where are you from, Mitchum?
FRANK:	Chicago. But I don't live there now.
POLICEMAN:	Where do you live?
FRANK:	Here. In New York.
POLICEMAN:	What's the address?
FRANK:	104 Spring Street.
POLICEMAN:	Do you have a job?
FRANK:	No, I don't. I don't work. I can't find a job.
POLICEMAN:	Hmm. Tell us about your parents—your mother and father.
FRANK:	I don't live with them.
POLICEMAN:	Where do they live?
FRANK:	My mother lives in Chicago.
POLICEMAN:	And your father?
FRANK:	I don't know. I think he lives in Las Vegas, but I'm not sure.
POLICEMAN:	OK. That's all for now. No more questions. Take him away!

2 Ask and answer questions about the burglar.

Does he {live / work} in ___?

Where does his {mother / father} ___?

Is he sure {his father / his mother} lives in ___?

3 Talk and write about the burglar.

1. ___ first name ___ ___.
2. ___ last ___ ___ Mitchum.
3. ___ ___ from ___.
4. He ___ live in Chicago.
5. His mother ___ in ___.
6. He doesn't ___ with her.
7. ___ thinks ___ father ___ in Las Vegas, but he isn't sure.
8. ___ address ___ 104 Spring Street.
9. He ___ ___ a job.
10. He ___ work.

10e

1 LISTEN

Here is Harry Gilmore again. What do you know about him? And what don't you know about him?

Harry doesn't work in a travel agency or a factory. He has a nightclub. It's called the Paradise Club. Harry owns it. It is his nightclub.

He doesn't live in an apartment. He lives in a big house and he owns a big car. He buys expensive clothes, drinks a lot of scotch and smokes a lot of cigars. He earns a lot of money, but he spends a lot of money too. He earns $100,000 a year. That is a lot of money, but Harry wants more! He wants more money.

He is looking at a photograph of Jackie Hunter. He knows her, but she doesn't know him. Jackie's father is very rich. Harry knows that too.

2

We can say this about Harry:
"He doesn't work in a factory."
But Harry says:
"I don't work in a factory."

What is Harry saying now?

1. He doesn't live in an apartment.
2. He doesn't own a small car.
3. He doesn't buy cheap clothes.
4. He doesn't get up at seven.
5. He doesn't run in Washington Square Park.
6. He doesn't teach English.
7. He doesn't know Bill Rivera.
8. He doesn't watch television every night.

3 What about you?

Are these things right or wrong?

You own a nightclub.   **That's right. I own a nightclub.**
OR
That's wrong. I don't own a nightclub.

1. You work in a nightclub.
2. You smoke a lot of cigars.
3. You earn $100,000 a year.
4. You steal things from houses.
5. You go to Columbia University.
6. You own four cars.
7. You understand ten foreign languages.
8. You live in an apartment in Greenwich Village.
9. You go to Shakespeare's every night.

10f

1 Look at the grammar: Simple Present

Harry	owns lives earns drinks smokes buys	a nightclub. in a big house. $100,000 a year. scotch every day. a lot of cigars. expensive clothes.

Bill Sue	doesn't	own live earn drink smoke buy	a nightclub. in a big house. $100,000 a year. scotch every day. a lot of cigars. expensive clothes.
I You We They	don't		

2 Write about Harry Gilmore.

1. Harry ___ a nightclub.
2. He ___ a big car.
3. He ___ in ___ big house.
4. He ___ rich.
5. He ___ $100,000 a year.

3 Do you remember Carol Lee? Can you write about her?

1. She ___ ___ a nightclub.
2. She ___ ___ a big car.
3. She ___ ___ in New York City.
4. Carol ___ in Rye.
5. She ___ in a travel agency.
6. She ___ ___ in a nightclub.

4 Here are Tom and Marie Williams again. Do you remember them?

1. They ___ in an apartment in New York City.
2. They ___ ___ in Rye.
3. They ___ ___ a nightclub.
4. Tom ___ in a factory, but he ___ earn $100,000 a year.
5. He ___ $22,000 a year.
6. Marie ___ in a travel agency and ___ $24,000 a year.

5 What is Bill Rivera saying?

1. I ___ ___ a nightclub and I ___ ___ $100,000 a year.
2. I ___ $16,000 a year.
3. I don't ___ a big car.
4. I don't ___ a lot of cigars and I ___ drink a lot of scotch.

6 Tom and Marie Williams are talking. What are they saying?

1. We ___ in an apartment in Greenwich Village.
2. We ___ ___ in a big house.
3. We don't ___ a big car.
4. We ___ smoke a lot of cigars or cigarettes.
5. We ___ drink a lot of scotch.

UNIT 11
Friday Evening

11a

1

LISTEN

Do you remember Pat? It's January now and it's very cold. Pat is in a coffee shop. He wants a cup of coffee. His money is in his hand.

PAT: A cup of coffee, please.
WAITER: Can you pay for it?
PAT: Of course I can! Here's my money! See?

2

Frank Mitchum is in prison now. He doesn't like the other prisoners. He doesn't like the food either.

FRANK: This food is terrible!
PRISONER: Can I have it? I'm hungry.
FRANK: Here, take it! I don't want it!

3

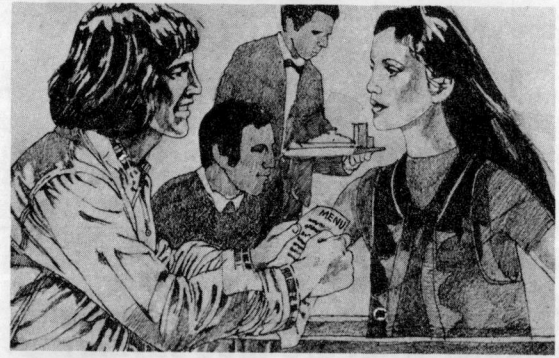

Mike and Jackie are having dinner in an Italian restaurant.

MIKE: Do you like pizza?
JACKIE: Yes, I do. I like it a lot.
MIKE: What kind do you want?
JACKIE: Hmm. Let's see. Pepper and mushroom, I think. Is that all right with you?
MIKE: Sure.

4

The Williams are having dinner at home. They're having steak and salad. Bobby isn't very hungry.

MARIE: What's wrong, Bobby? Don't you like your steak?
BOBBY: Yes, I like it. But I'm not very hungry. I can't finish it.
MARIE: All right.

11b

1 Look at the grammar: WANT/LIKE

He She	wants likes doesn't like	coffee. pizza. steak.

Mike is saying: "This pizza is good."
You can say: **He likes the pizza.**

Mike is saying: "This pizza is terrible!"
You can say: **He doesn't like the pizza.**

What can you say?

1. Jackie is saying: "This pizza is very good."
2. Frank is saying: "This food is terrible!"
3. Marie is saying: "This steak is very good!"
4. Tom is saying: "This salad isn't very good."

Pat is saying: "A cup of coffee, please."
You can say: **He wants a cup of coffee.**

What can you say now?

5. Sue is saying: "A tuna fish sandwich, please."
6. Mike is saying to the waiter: "A pizza with peppers and mushrooms, please."
7. Tom is saying: "A beer, please."
8. Bobby is saying: "A soda for me, please."

PICTURE ONE

1. Where is Pat?
2. What does he have in his hand?
3. He wants a cup of coffee. What is he saying?
4. What is the waiter's question?
5. What is Pat's answer?

PICTURE TWO

1. Where is Frank?
2. What is he doing?
3. What is he saying?
4. Does he like the other prisoners?
5. Does he like the food?
6. Look at the other man. Does he want Frank's food?

PICTURE THREE

1. Where are Mike and Jackie?
2. Does Jackie like pizza?
3. Which kind of pizza does she want?
4. Does Mike want pizza with peppers and mushrooms too?

PICTURE FOUR

1. What are the Williams doing?
2. Is Bobby hungry?
3. Does he like his steak?
4. Does he want it?

2 Jackie is talking about what she likes for breakfast. LISTEN

JACKIE: I usually have a cup of coffee and a glass of orange juice. I like orange juice in the morning. Sometimes I have an egg too. And I like toast with jelly.

3 What about you?

What do you like for { breakfast? / lunch? / dinner? }

I usually / Sometimes I { have .... I like .... }

58

11c

1 Look at the pictures. Do you know what these things are?

You can see four kinds of vegetables here. You can see four kinds of meat too. Meat comes from animals. The name of the animal and the name of the meat aren't always the same.

Look at the last four pictures. These things aren't meat. But they aren't vegetables either.

2 Ask people in your class:

Do you like .... ?
Do you ever eat .... ?

3 And how do you like these things? Answer like this:

boiled   **fried**   **roast**   **broiled**   **raw**

I like	broiled roast fried	chicken. beef.

I don't like	boiled fried raw	fish. eggs. carrots.

4 What about you?

I like .... I don't like ....
I usually eat .... I never eat ....
Sometimes I eat ....

11d

1 Jackie and Mike want to go to a movie. It starts at eight o'clock. It is seven ten now and they are in an Italian restaurant.

WAITER: Are you ready to order?
MIKE: Yes. We'd like a pizza with peppers and mushrooms, please.
WAITER: And to drink? Do you want anything to drink?
MIKE: Do you have any wine?
WAITER: Yes, we do. What kind of wine do you want?
MIKE: Uh . . . I don't know. Do you want any wine, Jackie?
JACKIE: No, thanks. Not for me. But I'd like a glass of water.
MIKE: OK. She'd like a glass of water and I'd like some red wine.
WAITER: How much? A bottle?
MIKE: Oh, no. Just a glass.
WAITER: All right. A pizza with peppers and mushrooms, a glass of red wine and a glass of water. Is that all?
MIKE: Yes. That's all.

It is seven fifty now.

WAITER: Finished?
JACKIE: Yes. Thank you.
WAITER: Anything else?

MIKE: Do you want any coffee, Jackie?
JACKIE: No. Look at the time, Mike. It's ten to eight.
MIKE: Can we have the check, please?
WAITER: Sure.
JACKIE: Here's some money, Mike. I want to pay for my dinner.
MIKE: Oh. OK. Thanks.

2 Answer the questions.

1. What kind of pizza do they want?
2. Does Jackie want any wine?
3. What does she want?
4. What kind of wine does Mike want?
5. How much wine does he want?
6. Does Jackie want any coffee?
7. Does Jackie pay for her dinner?

3 You are in a restaurant.
Ask the waiter:

Do you have **any**	pizza? red wine? cheese? beer? etc.	Yes, we do.
		No, I'm sorry. We don't.

Now look at page 59.
Ask the waiter more questions.

Do you have **any** { peas?
potatoes?
carrots?
etc.

Now order things from the waiter. Say:

I'd
We'd } like **some** ...., please.

60

11e

1 LISTEN

It's eleven o'clock at night and Jackie is watching the news. The man is talking about the weather. It is cold and it's snowing. Can you see all that snow?
Jackie is writing a letter too.

2 Read the letter. Then ask people in your class questions about it.

3 Open Dialog

You are a friend of Jackie's. You are calling her from San Francisco. It is eight o'clock at night in San Francisco.

JACKIE: Hello?
YOU: Hello? Is ___ Jackie?
JACKIE: Yes, ___ is.
YOU: Hi, Jackie. This is ___.
JACKIE: ___! Where ___ ___?
YOU: ___ in San Francisco. How ___ ___?
JACKIE: Oh, ___ fine. ___ you?
YOU: ___, thanks. I'm ___ the news now. I ___ see all the ___ in New York.
JACKIE: Yes. ___ snowing and ___ very cold here.
YOU: ___ ___ like New York?
JACKIE: Yes, ___ ___. And ___ ___ my apartment here. Oh! ___ ___ a new boyfriend.
YOU: ___ ___ name?
JACKIE: Mike. ___ a student too.
YOU: ___ ___ go to New York University Law School?
JACKIE: No, ___ ___. He ___ ___ Columbia University.

Monday, Jan. 16

Dear Dad,
It's about 11:00 at night and I'm sitting here watching the late news on television. The weather is bad here. It's snowing and it's very cold. Thank God my apartment is warm. I don't like cold weather. I can't stand it.
But I like New York a lot. I'm happy here. I think it's a wonderful city. I can go to the theater or the ballet and I can go to a different restaurant every night. The restaurants in New York are excellent and the food is always delicious.
I have a new boyfriend. His name is Mike Brodsky and he goes to Columbia University. He's studying engineering. He wants to be an engineer.
Well, that's all for now. Write soon.
Love,
Jackie

11f

1 Read the letter from Jackie to her father again. Then ask and answer these questions.

1. ___ she ___ television now?
2. ___ the weather good in New York?
3. ___ ___ snowing?
4. ___ Jackie like snow?
5. ___ ___ like New York?
6. ___ she ___ to the theater and ballet in New York?
7. ___ ___ like the restaurants in New York?
8. What ___ her boyfriend studying?
9. ___ Jackie's father know Mike?

2 This is a letter from Mike to his mother. Complete the letter.

___ Mom,

___ about twelve o'clock ___ night. ___ sitting here ___ ___ apartment and ___ ___ to the radio ___ happy here in New York. ___ ___ it's a wonderful city. ___ a new girlfriend. ___ ___ is Jackie Hunter and ___ ___ from San Francisco. She ___ ___ New York University Law School. ___ ___ all for now. Write ___.

___,
Mike

3 Read this menu.

Menu

ENTREES
Fried Chicken   Broiled Filet of Sole
Roast Lamb   Sirloin Steak
All entrees come with vegetables and potato

VEGETABLES
Peas   Baked Potato
Carrots   French Fries

DESSERT
Vanilla or Chocolate Ice Cream
Apple Pie
Cheese Cake

BEVERAGES
Beer, Wine, Coffee, Tea

4 Now order.

WAITER: ___ you ___ to order now?
YOU: Yes, ___ ___ the ___, please.
WAITER: What ___ of vegetable ___ you want?
YOU: ....
WAITER: ___ ___ want baked potato or french fries?
YOU: ....
WAITER: Anything to drink? Wine? Beer?
YOU: ....
WAITER: ___ that all?
YOU: ....

And now you want to pay.

YOU: ___ ___ the check, please?
WAITER: Sure.

UNIT 12
Saturday Morning

12a

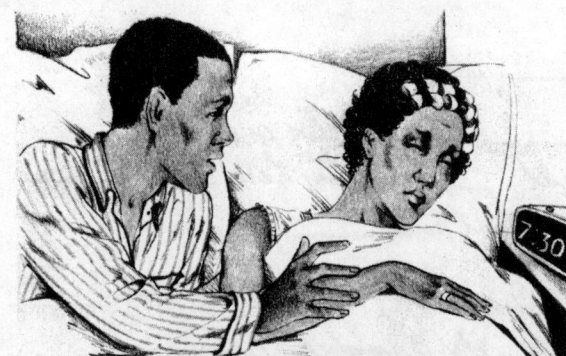

It is Saturday morning, February 26 (twenty-sixth).
It is exactly seven thirty in the morning.
Marie works on Saturdays. Tom doesn't.

TOM: Come on, Marie. Get up. It's seven thirty.
MARIE: Oh, I don't want to get up this morning. And I don't want to work today. I want to sleep!

It is eleven thirty now. Mike Brodsky wants to go to Shakespeare's. But Jackie wants to go to Washington Square Park.

MIKE: Let's go to Shakespeare's. Let's have a drink there.
JACKIE: No, I don't want to go there now. Let's go to the park. Look! The sun's shining! Come on!

Bobby Williams doesn't go to school on Saturdays. It is twelve o'clock now and he and his father are in Central Park. There is a zoo in Central Park.

BOBBY: Dad! I want to go to the zoo. I want to see the animals there!
TOM: All right. Let's go.

Do you remember Frank Mitchum? He is still in prison. He is standing at a window.
Frank wants to leave the prison. He wants to walk in the streets. He wants to go to bars, drink beer, sit in the sun and talk to women. But he can't.

12b

PICTURE ONE

1. Where are Tom and Marie?
2. What does Marie do on Saturdays?
3. What about Tom?
4. What is he saying to her?
5. And what is she saying to him?

PICTURE TWO

1. Where does Mike want to go?
2. What is he saying?
3. Does Jackie want to go there?
4. Where does she want to go?
5. What is she saying?

PICTURE THREE

1. What time is it now?
2. Where are Bobby and Tom?
3. What is Bobby saying?
4. Does Tom want to go to the zoo too?

PICTURE FOUR

1. *Talk about Frank Mitchum.*
   He wants to ....
2. *Ask and answer the question.*
   Can Frank .... ?
3. What is Frank saying?
   "I want to ...."

1 Look at the grammar: WANT TO

I We You They	want to	go to .... see .... have a .... sit in ....
He She	wants to	eat .... drink ....

2 Write these sentences.

Marie ___ to sleep. *Marie wants to sleep.*

1. She doesn't want ___ ___ up.
2. Bobby ___ ___ go to the zoo.
3. Tom ___ ___ ___ to the zoo too.
4. They ___ ___ see the animals there.
5. Mike is saying:
   "I ___ ___ ___ a drink at Shakespeare's."
6. But Jackie is saying:
   "I ___ ___ ___ to the park!"

3 Look at these sentences.

Let's { **go** to Shakespeare's.
have a drink there.
sit in the sun.
see the animals in the zoo. }

4 You are talking to a friend. You want to have a drink at Shakespeare's with your friend.

You can say:

"**Let's have a drink at Shakespeare's.**"

What can you say now? You want to:

1. go to Washington Square Park
2. go to a movie
3. watch television
4. listen to the radio
5. have dinner in a restaurant
6. go there now

12c

1 Mike and Jackie often go to a movie on Saturdays. They usually go in the evening. Here are six movies. They are playing in New York this week. 🎧 LISTEN

1

2

3

4

5

6

The six movies are different. What kind are they?

The first movie is a western.   The third one is a love story.   The fifth one is a disaster movie.
The second one is a war movie.   The fourth one is a horror movie.   The sixth is a comedy.

2 What about you?

1. What kind of movies do you like?
2. What about science fiction movies? Do you like them too?
3. Do you want to go to a movie tonight?
4. What kind of movie do you want to see?

12d

1 Now listen to Mike and Jackie.

JACKIE: Let's go to a movie tonight.
MIKE: OK. What do you want to see?
JACKIE: I don't know. What about you?
MIKE: Well, *The Last Bridge* is playing at the Waverly here in Greenwich Village.
JACKIE: It's a war movie, isn't it?
MIKE: Yeah.
JACKIE: I don't like war movies. I never go to them.
MIKE: Oh, well, here's a paper. You can see what's playing at the other movie theaters.
JACKIE: What about *A Star in the Night?*
MIKE: What kind of movie is it?
JACKIE: It's a kind of . . . love story. But Barbara Streiser is in it. She sings too. I think she's very good.
MIKE: I don't really like her. What else is playing?
JACKIE: Ah hah! Here's a movie for you. *Blood and the Vampire*. I know you like that kind of movie.
MIKE: A horror movie? No. Not tonight.
JACKIE: What about a western?
MIKE: Is there a good one playing?
JACKIE: What do you know about *The Sheriff?*
MIKE: Who's in it?
JACKIE: John Dane and Lauren Bacardi.
MIKE: Well, he's a good actor and she's a very good actress. Where's it playing?
JACKIE: At the Classic. Do you want to see it?
MIKE: OK. What time does it start?
JACKIE: Eight twenty.
MIKE: All right. Let's go.

2 Answer the questions.

1. What is *The Last Bridge?*
2. Does Jackie want to see it?
3. Where is it playing?
4. What is the Waverly?
5. Does Jackie want to see *A Star in the Night?*
6. What does she say about it?
7. What does she say about Barbara Streiser?
8. And what does Mike say about her?
9. What kind of movies does he like?
10. What does he want to see?
11. What about Jackie?
12. Who's in the movie and where is it playing?

3 Now talk about the conversation.

Jackie wants to .... tonight. They can see ....
It's playing at .... He/She wants to ....
He/She doesn't want to ....

4 Open Dialog

Bill Rivera and Sue Peterson are talking.

BILL: Let's ___ ___ a movie.
SUE: What ___ ___ to see?
BILL: *Blood and* ___ ___ .
SUE: No, I don't ___ ___ movies!
BILL: Well, what ___ *A Star* ___ ___ ___?
SUE: ___ in it?
BILL: Barbara Streiser.
SUE: And where's it ___?
BILL: ___ the Greenwich.
SUE: OK. ___ go. What time ___ ___ ___?
BILL: Eight thirty.

66

12e

1 Carol works at the travel agency on Saturdays. She is talking to a young married couple. Their names are Steve and Joyce. 🎧 LISTEN

JOYCE: We'd like some information, please. We want to go to Spain.
CAROL: OK. What do you want to know?
JOYCE: Well, first of all, we want to know the air fare to Madrid.
CAROL: When do you want to go?
STEVE: We don't really know. June, or maybe in July.
CAROL: I see. Well, in May and June the fare is $480. But it's less in March and April. It's only $460.
JOYCE: And what about July?
CAROL: It's more in July.
STEVE: More? How much is it then?
CAROL: It's $525.
STEVE: Oh . . .
JOYCE: Can you give us a brochure, please? We want to think about it.
CAROL: Of course. Here you are.
STEVE: Thanks.
CAROL: You're welcome.

2 Ask questions about Steve and Joyce. Give the answers too.

1. Where ___ they want ___ go?
2. ___ they ___ to ___ to Madrid in February?
3. ___ they ___ ___ go in March?
4. When ___ they ___ ___ go?

3 Now talk about the conversation.

1. Steve and Joyce want ___ ___ ___.
2. They ___ ___ go in ___ or maybe in ___.
3. The fare in ___ is ___.
4. But in ___ the fare ___ ___.

4 Now look at this information and answer the questions.

Round-Trip Fares New York—Madrid	
MAR 1 – APR 30	$460
MAY 1 – JUNE 30	$480
JULY 1 – SEPT 14	$525
SEPT 15 – OCT 31	$480
NOV 1 – FEB 28	$440

1. What is the fare in April?
2. Is it the same in May?
3. Is it more or is it less in August?

Now ask more questions.

What is the fare in ___?
Is it **more/the same/less** in ___?

12f

1 Look at the fares for September, October, November, December, January and February again.

JULY 1 – SEPT 14	$525
SEPT 15 – OCT 31	$480
NOV 1 – FEB 28	$440

Before September 15 the fare is $525, but after September 15 the fare is $480.

And after October 31, it's only $440!

2 Answer the questions.

1. What is the fare before September 15?
2. Is the fare the same after September 15?
3. Is it more?
4. What can you say about the fare after October 31?
5. You are going to Madrid after September 15 but before October 31. How much do you pay?

3 Here is some more information from the brochure. What does it tell you?

Round-Trip Fares New York—Paris		Round-Trip Fares New York—Athens	
MAR 1 – APR 30	$525	JULY 1 – SEPT 14	$760
MAY 1 – JUNE 30	$550	SEPT 15 – OCT 31	$680
JULY 1 – SEPT 30	$600	NOV 1 – FEB 28	$630

Talk about the fares.

Before ___ the fare to ___ is ___, but **after** ___ the fare is ___.

4 Open Dialog

You and a friend are talking to Carol now.

YOU: ___'d ___ some ___, please.
We ___ ___ ___ Athens.
CAROL: What ___ ___ ___ know?
YOU: Well, what ___ ___ air ___ to Athens ___ September?
CAROL: Well, ___ September 15 the ___ is $760, but ___ September 15 it's $680.
YOU: Oh. ___ ___ give ___ a brochure?
We ___ ___ ___ about it.
CAROL: Of course. ___ ___ ___ .

READING AND WRITING FOLLOW-UP: Units 10–12

1 Look at this brochure from Carol Lee's travel agency in Greenwich Village.

It is easy to get to Mexico from the United States and people often go there on vacation.

Tom Williams is going to Acapulco with his wife, Marie, and his son, Bobby. Bobby is under twelve. They want to stay in a moderate hotel for four days and three nights (from Friday to Monday). They want the American Plan.

How much do they have to pay?

Jackie Hunter wants to go to Acapulco for eight days and seven nights. She wants a deluxe hotel. She doesn't want the American Plan.

How much does she have to pay?

What about you?
You want to take a vacation in Acapulco too.
How long do you want to stay?
What kind of hotel do you want?
Do you want the American Plan or the European Plan?

How much does all this cost?

ACAPULCO HOLIDAYS

4 Days/3 Nights or 8 Days/7 Nights
in **Acapulco** at your choice of hotel

PACKAGE INCLUDES:
- Round-trip transportation between airport and hotel.
- Air-conditioned room with private bath.
- Half-day tour of the city.

Per Person Rates	European Plan*		American Plan**	
Hotel	3 Nights	7 Nights	3 Nights	7 Nights
★ Moderate	$140	$260	$215	$505
★★ First Class	200	400	300	645
★★★ Deluxe	250	500	375	800

*European Plan does not include meals
**American Plan includes breakfast and dinner

NOTE: Prices do not include air fare or service charges and taxes. Children under twelve are free (European Plan) when sharing accommodations with parents. For American Plan packages, add $22.00 per day for each child under twelve.

★ **Moderate**— near beach, telephone in every room, coffee shop, restaurant
★★ **First Class**— on the beach, telephone and TV in every room, coffee shop, restaurant, nightclub, room service
★★★ **Deluxe**— on the beach, telephone and color TV in every room, coffee shop, restaurants, disco, bar, room service, swimming pool, tennis courts

Make a reservation. Look at Jackie's letter. Then write a short letter to the Travel Center, 61 West 8th Street, New York, N.Y. 10011. Tell the travel agent where you want to go, when you want to go, how long you want to stay and what kind of hotel you want.

Address an envelope too.

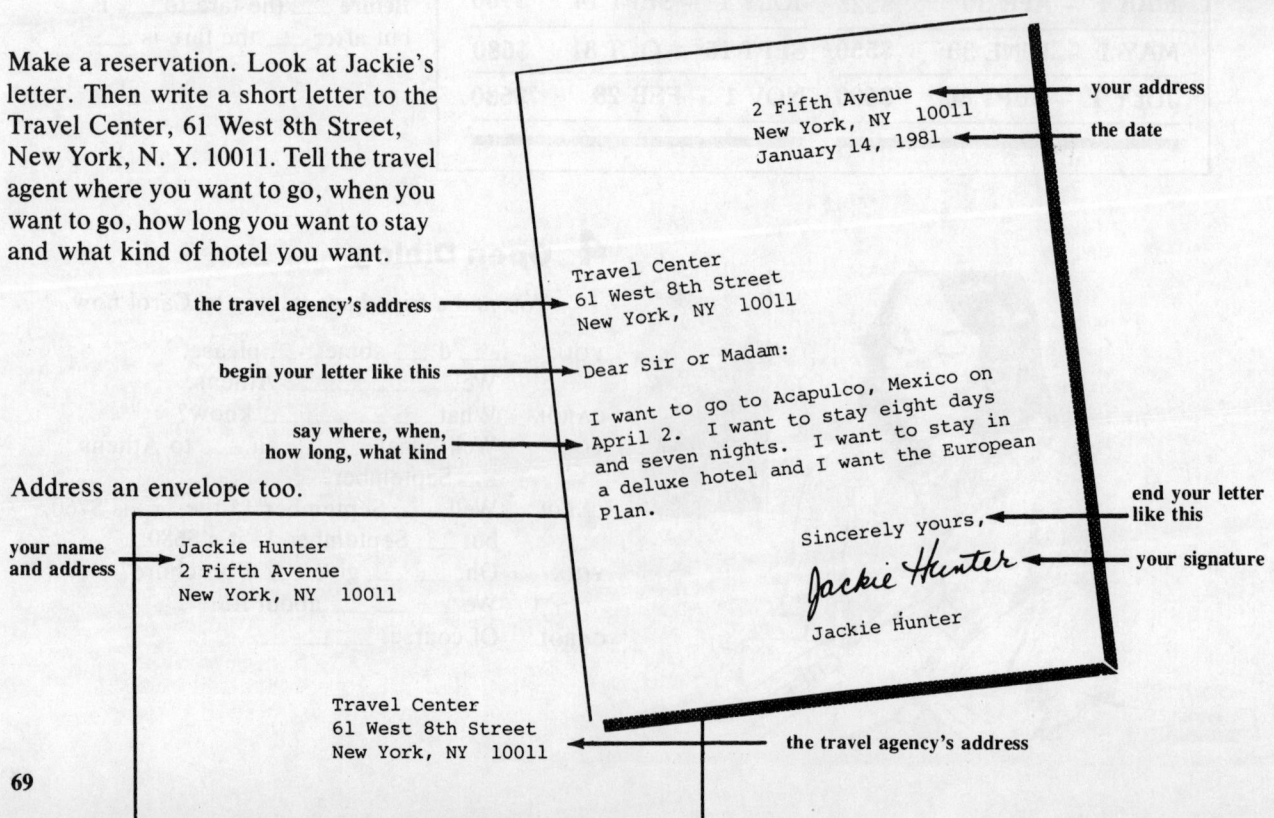

2 Look at this. It is from the Village News.

Now answer the questions.

1. The *Village News* thinks two movies are excellent. Which two movies?
2. You want to go to a movie. You only have $4.50. Which movie theaters can you go to?
3. It is one o'clock in the afternoon. You want to see a movie now. Which movie can you go to?
4. You're taking your brother to a movie. He wants to see a war movie. Which movie theater can you go to?

```
         * = Bad        *** = Good
        ** = Fair      **** = Excellent
```

CLASSIC
The Sheriff****
3:40, 6:00, 8:20
Late show Fri. and Sat. 10:40
Tickets $4.00

WAVERLY
The Last Bridge**
2:20, 5:20, 8:20
Tickets $5.00

GREENWICH
A Star in the Night***
3:25, 5:55, 8:30, 11:30
Tickets $5.00

CARLTON
Blood and the Vampire****
3:50, 6:15, 8:40
Tickets $4.50

GRANADA
The City Is Burning**
1:15, 4:30, 7:45, 11:15
Tickets $4.50

PLAZA
Laugh Now, Pay Later*
2:30, 4:15, 6:00, 8:15
Tickets $3.50

Martin Hunter
2172 PACIFIC, SAN FRANCISCO, CALIFORNIA 94115

January 25

Dear Jackie,

I'm in my new house now. It's very nice and I have a beautiful view of San Francisco Bay. I hope you can come and stay here next year.

It's raining and it's cold. I can't stand cold weather, but in a few weeks I'm going to Saudi Arabia. It's hot there. I'm going on business. Maybe I can stop and see you in New York on the way.

I see your mother sometimes, but not very often. Do you write to her? I hope so. I think she's happy now. I'm happy now too. This is the best thing for her and me. I hope you understand.

Love,
Dad

3 Read this letter from Jackie's father.

Ask and answer these questions about Mr. Hunter.

1. Where ___ ___ ___?
2. ___ ___ ___ a beautiful view of San Francisco Bay?
3. Is it ___ in San Francisco now?
4. Does he like ___ ___?
5. Is ___ ___ ___ Saudi Arabia in a few weeks?
6. ___ ___ hot there?
7. ___ ___ ___ there on business?
8. ___ ___ stop in New York ___ ___ ___?
9. ___ Mr. Hunter live ___ Mrs. Hunter?
10. ___ ___ happy now?

Address envelopes for these people.
Use: **Mr., Mrs.** *or* **Miss.**
(You can also use **Ms.**)

1. Jackie's father. His full name is Martin Hunter and his address is in his letter.
2. Jackie's mother, Marjorie Hunter. She lives at 908 South Curson Avenue, Los Angeles, California 90036.
3. Carol Lee. Her address is 134 Country Ridge Road, Rye, New York 10580.

UNIT 13 Frank's Last Day in Prison

13a

LISTEN

1

S	M	T	W	T	F	S
			1	2	3	4
5	6	7	8	9	10	11

(MARCH calendar shown: dates 1–31, with 31 circled)

Look at this calendar. It is March.
Today is Thursday, March 31 (thirty-first).
Yesterday was Wednesday, March 30 (thirtieth). Last month was February and the month before that was January.

2

It is nine o'clock in the morning. Frank Mitchum is in prison, but he is happy. He is happy because today is his last day in prison. The doors are opening.

GUARD: All right, Mitchum. You can leave now.
FRANK: Goodbye.
GUARD: I don't want to see you again.
FRANK: And I don't want to see *you* again either!

3

Harry Gilmore and Lucky Jones are outside the prison. They are there because they want to talk to Frank.

LUCKY: Look! There he is! He's coming now.
HARRY: Good! But I don't want to talk to him here. Follow him.

4

It is ten thirty now and Frank is in Washington Square Park. He was in prison at nine this morning. But now Frank is free. That's why he is smiling. He is smiling because he is free. Harry and Lucky are in the park too. Can you see them? They were outside the prison at nine this morning.

71

13b

PICTURE ONE

1. *Talk about the calendar you can see in the picture.*

   Today is ___, ___ ___.
   Yesterday was ___, ___ ___.
   Last month ___ ___.

2. *Now talk about your calendar.*

   Today ___ ___, ___ ___.
   Yesterday ___ ___, ___ ___.
   Last month ___ ___.

PICTURE TWO

1. What time is it?
2. Where is Frank?
3. Is he happy?
4. Why?

PICTURE THREE

Ask and answer the questions.

1. Where are ....?
2. Why are ....?
3. Is Frank .... now?
4. Does Harry want ....?

PICTURE FOUR

1. Where is Frank now?
2. Where was he at nine this morning?
3. Where are Harry and Lucky?
4. Where were they at nine?

1 Look at the grammar: Simple Past Tense of BE

I He She It	was	in ___	yesterday. last month. last year. at ___ o'clock this morning.
You They We	were		

2 Read this paragraph about Frank.

It **is** ten o'clock. Frank **is** in Washington Square Park. He **was** in prison at nine. He **was** there yesterday too. Harry and Lucky **are** in Washington Square Park now. They **were** outside the prison at nine this morning.

3 What about you?

1. Where were you yesterday?
2. Where were you last week?
3. And last month?
4. What about last year?

4 Answer the questions.

Yes, I was./No, I wasn't.

1. Were you in Washington Square Park yesterday?
2. Were you in Washington Square Park last year?
3. Were you in school yesterday?
4. Were you in school last week or last month?

5 Ask people in your class:

Were you	in Washington Square Park in the United States in school in ___	last year? last month? in 19___?
Where were you		in 19___? last year? at ___ o'clock yesterday?

13c

1 LISTEN

Frank is thinking. He doesn't know that Harry and Lucky are behind him.

"I'm free again! At nine o'clock this morning I was in prison, but I'm out now! I don't want to go back there. I wasn't happy there. Things were terrible.

"But what can I do now? I can't go back to Chicago because my mother doesn't want to see me. And I don't want to stay in New York because I don't have a job. And I don't have any money either.

"Maybe my father can help me. But where is he? Last year he was in Las Vegas, I think. And the year before that he was in Miami. But where is he now? I don't know.

"What about my sister? No, she can't help me either."

2 Ask questions about Frank. What are the answers?

1. Is he ___ now?
2. Was he ___ { yesterday? / last week? / last month? }
3. Does he have ___ ___?
4. Can his father ___ ___?
   Can his sister ___ ___?
5. Does his mother want to ___ ___?
6. Does he want to ___ ___ ___ ___?
7. Where was his father last ___?
   Where was his father ___ ___ ___ ___?

3 Now you are talking to Frank. Ask him questions.

1. Are you ___ ___?
2. Were you ___ ___?
3. Do you have a ___?
   Do you have any ___?
4. Where is your ___?
5. Can he ___ ___?
   Can she ___ ___?
6. ___ your mother want to ___ ___?
7. Where was your father last ___?

4 Talk and write about Frank.

1. Frank was ....
2. He is ....
3. He doesn't have ....
4. His mother ....
5. His father ....
6. His sister ....

5 What about you?

Do you have a	brother? sister?

Where was	he she	last year? last month?

73

13d

1 Harry and Lucky want to talk to Frank. But why?

LUCKY: Hello, Frankie. How are you?
FRANK: Lucky! What are you doing here? Harry! You're here too. But . . .
LUCKY: We were outside the prison this morning. At nine o'clock.
FRANK: Were you? But I didn't see you.
HARRY: No, but we saw you. And we followed you. We want to talk to you, Frank.
FRANK: Why? What do you want?
LUCKY: Let's go to Harry's house.
FRANK: Go to Harry's house? Why?
HARRY: Because we want to talk to you!
LUCKY: We have a job for you, Frankie.
HARRY: And there's money in it.
FRANK: A job? Money? What are you talking about? Look! Why are you here? Come on! Tell me!
HARRY: We can't. Not here.
LUCKY: That's why we want to go to Harry's house. We want to talk about the job.
FRANK: Look! I . . . I don't want to talk to you about a job! No more jobs for me! Not with you.
LUCKY: Not with us? Why?
FRANK: Because I don't want to go back to prison again! That's why.
HARRY: Don't you want to know more about the job?

FRANK: No! I don't want to know anything about the job! I'm leaving! Goodbye!
LUCKY: Frankie boy! Stop! Talk to us! Listen!
HARRY: That's all right, Lucky. He doesn't want to talk to us now. But wait! Just wait!

2 Answer the questions.

1. Does Frank know Lucky?
2. Does he know Harry too?
3. Does he want to talk to them?
4. What do they want to do?
5. Why do they want to talk to him?
6. What does Harry say about the job?
7. Does Frank want to know about the job?
8. Does he want to work with Harry and Lucky?
9. Why doesn't he want to work with them?

3 Ask questions with WHY . . . . ?

You are Frank. Lucky says:
   "We want to talk to you."

You say:
   "Why do you want to talk to me?"

Lucky says:

1. We want to see you.
2. We want to go to Harry's house.
3. We want to tell you about a rich girl.
4. We watch her.
5. We follow her.
6. We're going to her apartment now.

4 Talk and write about Lucky, Harry and Frank.

1. At nine o'clock Lucky and Harry ___ ___ ___ ___.
2. They saw ___, but Frank didn't ___ ___.
3. They ___ him to Washington Square Park.
4. Now they want to ___ ___ ___.
5. But Frank doesn't want ___ ___ ___ ___.
6. He doesn't want to ___ ___ ___ because ....

13e

1 LISTEN

Let's learn more about Frank.

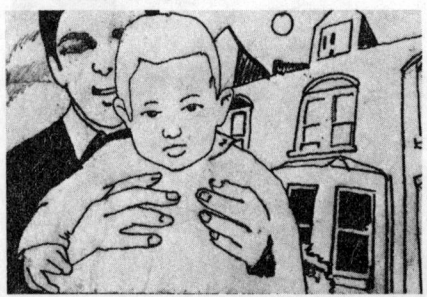

Frank was born in Chicago. His mother was a waitress and his father was a bus driver. They were born in Chicago too.

Frank started school when he was five. He was in school for eleven years.

He wasn't very happy at school. And he wasn't a very good student either. He left school when he was sixteen.

His first job was in a supermarket. He was there for two years. His next job was in a factory.

He came to New York when he was eighteen. He worked in a supermarket in New York too. He went to prison last year.

He is twenty years old now. He was in prison for three months, but he is free now.

2 What is Frank saying?

1. I ___ born ___ .
2. My parents ___ born ___ ___ ___ .
3. My mother ___ ___ ___ and my father ___ ___ ___ ___ .
4. I started school when ___ ___ ___ .
5. I ___ very happy at school.
6. I left school when ___ ___ ___ .
   etc.

3 Now talk and write about yourself.

1. I ___ born in ___ .
2. My parents ___ born ___ ___ .
3. I started ___ when I ___ .
4. I left ___ when I ___ .
5. My first job ___ in a ___ .

13f

1 Look at these questions and answers.

Was Frank born in Chicago?	Yes, he **was**.
Was Jackie born there?	No, she **wasn't**.
Were Frank's parents born there?	Yes, they **were**.
Were Jackie's parents born there?	No, they **weren't**.
Where **were** you born?	I **was** born in ___.
Where **were** your parents born?	They **were** born in ___.

2 Ask and answer these questions about Frank.

1. Where ___ Frank born?
   He ___ ___ in Chicago.
2. ___ his parents born there too?
   Yes, ___ ___.
3. ___ Frank happy at school?
   No, ___ ___.
4. ___ ___ a very good student?
   ___, ___ ___.
5. Where ___ his first ___?
   ___ a supermarket.
6. And ___ ___ ___ next job?
   ___ a factory.
7. Where ___ the factory?
   ___ ___.
8. How old ___ he when he ___ to New York?
   ___ ___ ___.

3 Open Dialog

You are asking Frank questions.

1. YOU: ___ ___ ___ ___?
   FRANK: Me? In Chicago.
2. YOU: ___ ___ ___ ___ ___ too?
   FRANK: Yes, they were.
3. YOU: ___ ___ a very good student?
   FRANK: Well, I wasn't a very good student and I wasn't a very bad student either.
4. YOU: ___ ___ ___ first job?
   FRANK: My first job? In a supermarket in Chicago.
5. YOU: How old ___ ___ when you ___ to New York?
   FRANK: I was 18. I'm 20 now. But tell me something now! Why are you asking all these questions?

UNIT 14
Carol's Old Job

14a

This is Carol Lee again. Do you remember her? She lives in Rye with her father. She works in a travel agency now. Marie Williams is her boss. Carol likes her job and she is happy. She starts work at nine and finishes at five thirty.

But things were different last year. Last year she worked in an office. She typed letters all day. Her boss was a man named Mr. Carson.
She started at eight thirty and finished at five.
Carol lived in Rye then too.

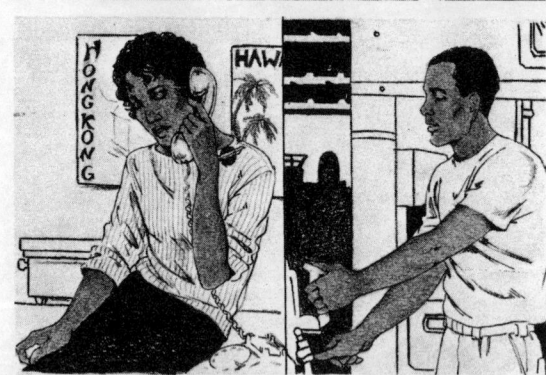

Marie Williams works in a travel agency and Tom Williams works in a factory in New York. Things were the same last year.
But what about before that?

Before they came to New York, Tom and Marie lived in Cleveland. They worked there too. Cleveland is a city in Ohio.
Tom worked in a big factory in Cleveland. Marie worked in a small travel agency there. She managed the agency. She manages the agency in Greenwich Village too.

14b

1

CAROL: I live in Rye now. I lived there last year too. But last year I worked in an office, and now I work in a travel agency.

PICTURE ONE

Ask and answer the questions.

1. Does ___ ___ with her father?
2. Where .... ?
3. ___ ___ like ___ ?
4. ___ ___ happy?
5. What ___ ___ ___ start work?
6. ___ ___ ___ ___ finish ___ ?

PICTURE TWO

Now talk about last year.

1. Last year Carol ___ ___ an office.
2. ___ ___ letters.
3. Her boss ___

PICTURE THREE

What questions can you ask about Tom and Marie this year?

PICTURE FOUR

Can you ask questions about Tom and Marie before they came to New York?

Did	Tom Marie	work in ___ ? live in ___ ?
Yes,	he she	did.
No,	he she	didn't.

2 Talk and write about yourself.

Where did you live last year?
Where do you live now?
Do you have a job now? Where do you work?
Did you work last year? Where?

I **live** in ___ now and last year I **lived** in ___.
I **worked** in ___ last year and now I **work** in ___.

I don't have a job now, but **last year/in 19___/last month**, I worked in ___.

3 Ask people in your class:

Where **did** you	**live** **work**	in 19___? last year? last November?

Last ___ In 19___	I	**worked** **lived**	in ___.

14c

1 Carol is talking about her old job and her new job.

CAROL: Last year I worked in an office in Rye. That was before I got a job in a travel agency in Greenwich Village.

We started at eight thirty every morning and we finished at five. We had an hour for lunch.

The salary wasn't very good. I only earned $140 a week, and I wasn't very happy there.

My boss was a man named Mr. Carson. He was nice and I liked him. But the work wasn't interesting. I mean, I typed letters all day and answered the phone.

One day I bought a newspaper and saw an ad. A travel agency in Greenwich Village wanted someone with two foreign languages. Of course, I can speak Chinese. I can also speak Spanish and Italian. I studied them in college. I went to the travel agency and saw Marie Williams. She asked me some questions and then she gave me the job.

I earn more money at my new job. I think it's interesting. I'm happy there.

14d

1 Talk and write about Carol.

1. Last year Carol ___ in an office, but now she ___ in a travel agency.
2. Carol ___ happy at her old job, but now she ___ very happy.
3. At her old job, she ___ letters all day and ___ the phone.
4. She ___ at eight thirty every morning and ___ at five.
5. She ___ an hour for lunch at her old job.
6. One day she ___ a newspaper and ___ an ad.
7. She ___ to the travel agency and ___ Marie Williams.
8. Marie ___ her a lot of questions and Carol ___ them.
9. Marie ___ her the job.
10. At her old job Carol ___ $140 a week.
11. She ___ more now. Her salary ___ $180 a week.
12. She ___ at nine now and ___ at five thirty. And she ___ an hour for lunch.

2 Look at the grammar: Simple Present and Simple Past

Simple Present

| I You We They | work live start finish type answer want like | He She | works lives starts finishes types answers wants likes |

Simple Past (yesterday, last week, etc.)

| I You We They He She | worked lived started finished typed answered wanted liked |

These are *regular verbs*.

| I You We They | go come leave buy give think see have get | He She | goes comes leaves buys gives thinks sees has gets |

| I You We They He She | went came left bought gave thought saw had got |

And these are *irregular verbs*.

14e

1 LISTEN

It is Wednesday, April 13 now. Frank got out of prison last month. He is having an interview for a job.

MAN: Do you mind if I ask you some questions?
FRANK: No, that's all right.
MAN: Where did you go to school, Frank?
FRANK: In Chicago. I was born there.
MAN: When did you leave school?
FRANK: When I was sixteen.
MAN: What subjects did you study?
FRANK: What subjects?
MAN: Yes. Did you study math? Any foreign languages?
FRANK: Well . . . I studied math . . . yeah . . . and . . . Spanish and, uh . . . history. You know . . . the usual things.
MAN: What subjects did you like?
FRANK: Like? Oh . . . uh . . . English. I liked English. But I didn't like math.
MAN: And Spanish? Did you like Spanish?
FRANK: Well, it was . . . all right. You know.
MAN: Were you good at it?
FRANK: Well, you know, I was . . . all right. Not good. Not bad. It wasn't very interesting.
MAN: Hmmm. And when did you come to New York?
FRANK: When I was eighteen.
MAN: Where did you work?
FRANK: In a supermarket. I . . . uh . . . I left in December . . . last year.

MAN: Oh? Why did you leave the job? And what did you do then?
FRANK: Well, I left because . . . because . . . I went to prison.
MAN: What? You went to prison?
FRANK: Yeah. I got out last month.
MAN: Oh. Hmm. I see. I see.

2 Talk and write about Frank.

1. He ___ school ___ ___ ___ sixteen.
2. He studied ___, ___ and ___.
3. He liked ___.
4. He didn't like ___.
5. ___ ___ to New York when he was eighteen.
6. He ___ in a supermarket.
7. ___ ___ in December.
8. He ___ to prison in December and ___ ___ out last month.

3 What about you?

Where did you go to school?
What subjects did you study?
What subjects did you like?

Were you good at { math?
history?
foreign languages?

When did you leave school?

4 Ask people in your class:

Did you study ___?
Were you good at ___?
When did you leave school?
etc.

14f

1 Look at the grammar: Simple Past

I **went** to ....
Frank **worked** in a supermarket.
Jackie **came** to New York.
You **bought** a ....
We **saw** ....
Tom and Marie **wanted** ....

Yes/No Questions

Did	I **go** ___? he **work** in a supermarket? she **come** to New York? you **buy** ___? we **see** ___? they **want** ___?

Short Answers

Yes,	I he she	**did.**
No,	we you they	**didn't.**

2 Read this about Sue Peterson and Bill Rivera.

Sue got up at seven o'clock yesterday. She went to work at nine. She walked to work. She had lunch at one o'clock. She finished work at five thirty. In the evening she watched television and listened to the radio.

Bill Rivera ate dinner in a Chinese restaurant last night. Then he went to a movie. He saw a western. He liked it very much.

3 Now talk and write about Sue and Bill.

1. What time ___ Sue ___ up yesterday?
   She ___ up at seven.
2. ___ she ___ to work at eight?
   No, ___ ___ .
3. What time ___ she ___ to work?
   She ___ to work at nine.
4. ___ she ___ lunch at twelve?
   No, she ___ lunch at one.
5. ___ she ___ to a movie last night?
   No, ___ ___ .
6. ___ Bill ___ to a movie?
   Yes, ___ ___ .

4 Ask people in your class:

1. What time ___ ___ ___ up yesterday?
2. What time ___ ___ ___ to work/school?
3. ___ you ___ lunch at one o'clock too?
4. ___ you ___ television last night?
5. ___ you ___ to the radio?

5 What about you?

1. I ___ up at ___ .
2. I ___ to work/school at ___ .
3. I ___ lunch at ___ .
4. Last night I ....

UNIT 15
A Job for Frank

15a

Look at the date. It is Thursday, April 14.
What did Frank Mitchum do yesterday?
He got up at seven. He took a shower and shaved. Then he had breakfast. After that he went out and bought a newspaper.

He saw an ad in it. The ad said: "Radio factory needs part-time & full-time employees." There were a lot of ads in the paper. But Frank wanted to know more about the job in the radio factory.

Frank took a bus to the factory. He sat down in a big room and waited. There were a lot of other people in the room. They all wanted to work in the factory too.

Then a man came into the room and said, "Follow me, please." They went to an office and sat down. The man asked Frank a lot of questions. Frank answered them.

Frank wasn't happy when he came out of the factory. The man didn't give Frank a job because Frank got out of prison last month. He can't find a job because he was in prison. Frank is very unhappy today. He was unhappy yesterday too.

15b

Say why these things are wrong.

Yesterday was Tuesday.

> No! Yesterday was Wednesday.

1. Frank got up at eight yesterday.
2. Then he had lunch.
3. He went out and bought a magazine.
4. Frank went to a supermarket.
5. The job was in a shoe factory.
6. He sat down in a small room.
7. They all wanted to buy radios in the factory.
8. A woman interviewed Frank.
9. Frank asked a lot of questions.
10. The man answered them.
11. Frank was happy when he came out.
12. The man gave Frank the job.
13. Frank got out of prison yesterday.

1 Frank is telling you what he did yesterday. Complete the sentences.

1. ___ ___ ___ at seven.
2. Then I ___ ___ ___ and ___.
3. After that I ___ ___.
4. Then ___ ___ ___ ___ ___ a newspaper.
   etc.

2 Open Dialog

You are asking Frank questions about yesterday.

YOU: ___ ___ ___ ___ ___ ___ ?
FRANK: At seven.
YOU: ___ ___ ___ ___ ___ ___ ?
FRANK: Yes, of course I took a shower and shaved! What a question! And after that I went out and bought a newspaper.
YOU: Why ___ ___ ___ ___ ___ ?
FRANK: Because I wanted to find a job.

Now go on. Can you ask more questions about yesterday? What are the answers?

3 Ask people in your class about yesterday.

What time / When	did you	get up? have breakfast? go to work/school? go home?

What did you do	before	breakfast? you went to ___ ?
	after	you got home? dinner?

84

15c

1 This is a page from Tom Williams' appointment book. He did these things last week.

2 What did Tom do last week?

He ___ ___ ___ on Monday.
The plane ___ at ___ and
___ in Boston at ___.
On Tuesday he ....
etc.

Now ask questions about Tom.

Did he .... on Monday?
When did .... ?
What time did .... ?
What did .... on ___ ?

APRIL 1981

Go to Boston, plane leaves 8:30, arrives 9:20	MONDAY 4
See manager of new factory, have dinner with manager and his wife	TUESDAY 5
Return to New York (plane leaves 9:00, arrives New York 9:50)	WEDNESDAY 6
Buy new machines for factory	THURSDAY 7
Put ad in paper for new secretary	FRIDAY 8
SATURDAY 9 Go to zoo with Bobby	SUNDAY 10 Have lunch with Marie's mother

3 These two tickets were in Sue Peterson's purse. As you can see, they are old tickets.

Ask and answer questions about the concert ticket.

When ___ the concert?
When did Sue ___ to the concert?
Where ___ she sit?
How much ___ she pay for the ticket?
What time ___ the concert start?

Now ask questions about the train ticket.

Where .... ?
When .... ?
How much .... ?

15d

1 Bill Rivera is telling his class a story. It is a story about himself and Sue Peterson.

Last night I met my girlfriend at eight o'clock and we went to a movie. We saw a comedy. Burt Reynolds was in it. We liked it very much. It ended at ten o'clock.

After the movie we went to a Chinese restaurant. Then we walked home. My girlfriend . . . her name is Sue . . . and I had a cup of coffee at her apartment. We talked about the movie. I left her apartment at about midnight and walked home.

But when I got home, my keys weren't in my pocket. Well, what did I do? I climbed through a window. But one of my neighbors saw me. He thought I was a burglar. You see, there was a burglar in my apartment last December. He called the police. I was in bed when they came.

I found my keys this morning. They were in the pocket of another jacket.

2 Talk and write about Bill.

Last night Bill ....

3 You are talking to Bill. Ask him questions about last night.

What ....?
What kind ....?
Why ....? Did ....?
Where ....?
When ....?

15e

1 These are regular verbs.

walk	I **walked** to my friend's apartment last night.
watch	We **watched** a movie on TV.
start	It **started** at 9:00.
end	It **ended** at 10:30.
like	I **liked** it very much.
call	Later I **called** my mother.
talk	We **talked** about the movie.

And these are irregular verbs.

go	My friend and I **went** to a movie last night.
meet	We **met** outside the theater.
see	We **saw** an old western.
leave	We **left** the movie theater at about 10:00.
eat	We **ate** dinner in an Italian restaurant.
drink	We **drank** some wine with dinner.
have	Then we **had** some coffee.
take	I **took** the bus home.
get	I **got** home at about midnight.
find	I **found** a letter in my mailbox.
sit/read	I **sat** down and **read** it.

2 Write these sentences in the simple past.

Carol _____ (have) a busy day yesterday. She _____ (go) to work by train yesterday. It _____ (come) at 8:00. She _____ (get on) and _____ (sit down). She _____ (see) a friend on the train. They _____ (talk) about work and things like that. She _____ (get off) at Grand Central Station and _____ (take) a bus to the travel agency. Then she _____ (start) work. She _____ (finish) at 5:30. At 6:00 she _____ (meet) some friends near Lincoln Center. They _____ (have) dinner in a small Italian restaurant.

3 What about you?

1. What time do you usually get up?
2. What do you usually have for breakfast?
3. When do you usually leave for school or work?
4. Where do you usually have lunch?
5. What time do you usually get home?
6. What do you usually do in the evening? (watch TV? meet some friends?)

4 Now Carol is telling you what she did yesterday.

I ___ a busy day yesterday. I ___ ___ by ___. When it ___, I ___ on and ___ down. I ___ a friend ___ ___. We ___ about ___ ___ ___ ___. I ___ off at Grand Central Station and ___ a bus to the travel agency. Then I ___ ___. I ___ at 5:30 and at 6:00 I ___ two friends near Lincoln Center. We ___ dinner in ___ ___ ___ ___.

5 Now talk about what you did yesterday.

I ___ up at ___.
I ___ ___ for breakfast.
I ___ to school/work at ___.
I started/finished at ___.
Then I ....

15f

1 What about Frank? He can't find a job and he is very unhappy. He is sitting in the park again. Someone wants to talk to him. Who? **LISTEN**

LUCKY: Hello, Frankie boy. Do you mind if I sit down?
FRANK: Oh, it's you again, Lucky.
LUCKY: I saw you yesterday, Frankie. I followed you to that factory.
FRANK: What? You followed me? Why?
LUCKY: Because we're very interested in you, Frankie. Well, did you find a job? Did they give you a job yesterday?
FRANK: I think you know the answer.
LUCKY: Yeah, of course I do. Well, you can work for us, you know.
FRANK: Look! Do you mind if I ask you something?
LUCKY: No, sure. Go ahead, kid.
FRANK: You always talk about a job. But what is it?
LUCKY: I can't tell you that. But I can tell you this. There's a lot of money in it. I told you that when I saw you here before. Do you want to know more? Are you interested?
FRANK: I . . . I . . .
LUCKY: Because if you want to know more, I mean if you're really interested, Harry can tell you more. And he's waiting in a bar. Are you coming?
FRANK: Yeah . . . all right. Let's go.

2 Answer the questions.

1. What did Lucky do yesterday?
2. And what did Frank do?
3. What are they doing now?
4. Where are they going?
5. Why are they going there?

3 Ask the questions and then write them.

Frank wants to sit down. He says:
"Do you mind if I sit down?"

What do you say?

1. You want to open the window.
2. You want to make a phone call.
3. You want to smoke a cigarette.
4. You want to leave class early.
5. You want to close the door.
6. You want to ask some questions.

4 What do you think?

Harry and Lucky want to give Frank a job. What is the job? Maybe this information can help you.

Harry Gilmore wants more money. He sees a rich girl in the park every day. He knows her father is the president of a bank in San Francisco. Who is the girl? Why is Harry interested in her? What does he want to do?

READING AND WRITING FOLLOW-UP: Units 13–15

Shakespeare's: Favorite Student "Hangout"

In New York, bars are usually open every day. They can open at eight o'clock in the morning and stay open until four o'clock in the morning. Shakespeare's is a bar in New York. It's in Greenwich Village near the American Language Center. Bill Rivera goes there. Many other teachers and students go there too. It's their local "hangout." It's a friendly place and it's always busy.

Shakespeare's isn't open every day. It's closed on Sundays. And Shakespeare's doesn't open at eight o'clock. It opens at eleven o'clock. Dan Franklin is the owner of Shakespeare's. He likes his job, but he works very hard. Two other men help him.

In New York children under 18 cannot drink alcohol and they cannot go into bars. In Shakespeare's there is a sign over the bar. It says:

> **SORRY!**
>
> **We do not serve anyone under 18.**

Dan Franklin likes children. He has two children himself. But he is happy that children cannot come into his bar. "People come here to talk and have a quiet drink," he says, "They don't want children in here. They make too much noise."

1 Ask and answer these questions.

Are _bars usually open_ every day in New York?.
    Yes, they are.

1. What time ___ ___?
2. Where ___ ___?
3. Does Bill Rivera ___ ___?
4. Do other teachers and students ___ ___ too?
5. Is Shakespeare's ___ ___ Sundays?
6. ___ ___ does Shakespeare's open?
7. Who is the owner ___ ___?
8. Does he ___ ___ ___?
9. Can children under 18 ___ ___ ___?
10. ___ children under 18 ___ alcohol?

What about your country?

1. Do you have bars in your country?
2. If you don't, where can you drink coffee or tea in the evening?
3. What time do these places open and close?
4. What can you drink in them?
5. Can children under 18 go into them? What do they drink?

Start: **In my country**...............

2 Frank Mitchum looked at these ads for jobs in the paper. Can you understand them?

Which jobs aren't right for Frank?

This job isn't right for him because
he { can't ....
isn't ....
doesn't have experience in this kind of job. }

What about you?
Which jobs are right for you? Which jobs are wrong for you? Why?

You have to interview a person in your class for one of these jobs.
Ask questions like:
Can you ___? Do you ___? Do you have ___ ___? Are you ___?
Can you ask more questions?

VOCABULARY
Staff: the people working in an office, store, school, factory, etc.
Salary: the money you get for your work
Full-time: usually 40 hours of work a week
Experience: if you did this kind of work before, you have *experience*.
Part-time: less than full time

What are the other words you don't understand? Ask your teacher:
What does ___ mean?

THE VILLAGE NEWS Thursday, April 14, 1981

BARTENDER wanted for popular Greenwich Village bar. Good salary. 6 days a week. Apply in person at Shakespeare's, 58 West 8th Street.

COOK Saudi Arabia 170 miles from Jeddah. Salary $1200/mo., tax free. Free accommodations and food. Two trips home a year. For more information call Mr. Cardin 764-1045.

FULL-TIME SALES ASSISTANT for boutique. Experience necessary. $145-160/wk. For interview call Linda Field 581-8181.

MENSWEAR SALESPERSON 5-day week. 2 weeks vacation. Good salary. Apply KENT'S, 1263 Fifth Avenue or call 485-7844.

PARKING LOT ATTENDANT Quick Park 245 West 45th. Call Fred 836-6030.

RESTAURANT $200/WEEK. Young and beautiful staff for late night restaurant. Call 936-7801.

SECRETARY, part time or full time. Call Mr. Belden 485-6975.

SUPERMARKET Young person wanted for Greenwich Village supermarket. No experience necessary. Call Mr. Cardona 485-3271.

Teacher of English as a Second Language. University degree in ESL necessary. Salary $14,500 a year. Apply Pamela Dickinson, American Language Center, 450 Sixth Avenue, NYC 10011

Travel Agency. Good opportunity for man or woman with foreign languages. 485-5677.

ARE YOU BETWEEN 18 AND 50? Can you speak a foreign language? Do you want to travel? Can you work long hours for a very good salary? Do you have a driver's license? We are a big international organization and we are looking for people like you. Write to this paper, Box 790, for more information.

---

3 This is an answer to one of these ads. Which ad?

What about you?

Can you write a letter for this job too?
Give your name and other information.
What questions do you ask about the job?

---

18 East 66th Street
New York, N.Y. 10021
April 15, 19--

Box 790
The Village News
New York, N.Y. 10011

Dear Sir or Madam:

I saw your ad yesterday and I would like some more information.

What kind of job is it and where is your office? What are the hours and how much is the salary?

I am 26 years old and I work in an international bank. I can speak Spanish and French. I also have a driver's license. I want to travel and use my foreign languages. I can come to an interview next week.

Sincerely,

Suzanne Busch
Suzanne Busch

UNIT 16
The Kidnapping

16a

1

It is Friday night, May 20. Mike is waiting for Jackie in front of a movie theater. He got there on time. The movie is starting now, but Jackie isn't there. Mike is thinking.

MIKE: I don't understand it. Jackie's never late. Why isn't she here? What's the matter?

2

It is almost midnight now. Mike is calling Jackie. Mike saw the movie, but he didn't see all of it. It started at 8:30. He waited for half an hour. Then he went in. Jackie didn't see the movie. She didn't come to the theater.

MIKE: No answer! Where is she? Why didn't she come? What's the matter with her?

3

It is Saturday morning now. Mike is calling again. He called last night, but Jackie didn't answer then. And she isn't answering now.

MIKE: No answer again! And she didn't answer last night. Where can she be? I'm worried! I'm very worried!

4

This is Jackie's bed. She didn't sleep in it last night. She didn't go to the movie last night either. She wasn't in her apartment. She didn't come home. She ran in Washington Square Park yesterday morning. But she didn't come back. She didn't have breakfast. She didn't listen to Andrea Steele's radio program. She didn't go to school.

16b

1 Look at the grammar: Simple Past (Negative)

I You He She We They	didn't	go to a movie answer the phone see a western have breakfast run in Washington Square Park get there on time	yesterday. last week.

PICTURE ONE

Ask and answer the questions.

1. Where is ___?
2. Is the movie ___?
3. Is Jackie ___?
4. Is she often ___?

PICTURE TWO

1. What is Mike doing now?
2. Why?
3. Is Jackie answering?
4. *Ask and answer the questions.*
   Did Jackie ....?
   Did Mike ....?

PICTURE THREE

1. What did Mike do last night?
2. What is he doing now?
3. He is worried. Why?
4. What is he saying?

PICTURE FOUR

Ask and answer the questions.

1. Did Jackie ___ ___ yesterday?
2. Was she in her ___?
3. ___ ___ ___ in Washington Square Park?
4. ___ ___ ___ to Andrea Steele's radio program?
   etc.

2 Talk and write about Mike and Jackie.

Mike did these things yesterday. But Jackie didn't.

Example: Mike went to a movie.

Jackie didn't go to a movie.

1. He got there at 8:30.
2. He waited.
3. He went into the theater.
4. He went to a bar after the movie.
5. He saw Bill Rivera.
6. He talked to him.
7. He had a drink.
8. He went home.
9. He slept in a bed last night.

Now ask questions about Jackie.

Why didn't she ....?

Example: Mike went to a movie (but Jackie didn't).

Why didn't she go to a movie?

1. Mike got there on time.
2. He saw the movie.
3. He went home.
4. He slept in a bed.
5. He got up the next morning.
6. He had breakfast.
7. He took a shower.

3 Talk and write about yourself.

Did you do these things yesterday?

Example: see a movie

I saw a movie yesterday.
OR *I didn't see a movie yesterday.*

1. go to work
2. go to school
3. smoke two packs of cigarettes
4. have dinner in a restaurant
5. watch television
6. see a movie
7. have a drink in a bar
8. sleep in a bed
9. sleep in prison

16c

1 It is Saturday afternoon. Mike is calling Sue.

MIKE: Hello, Sue? This is Mike.
SUE: Oh, hi, Mike. How are things?
MIKE: Well, I'm worried about Jackie.
SUE: Worried about Jackie? Why? What's the matter with her?
MIKE: I don't know.
SUE: I'm sorry, Mike. I don't understand. What do you mean?
MIKE: Well, you see, we had a date last night. I mean, we wanted to see a movie, but she didn't come.
SUE: Yeah? And did you call her?
MIKE: Yes, I did. But she didn't answer. I called last night, and I called again this morning.
SUE: Oh, well, she . . .
MIKE: Listen, please. So after I called this morning, I went to her apartment. I knocked on the door. She didn't answer then either. I mean, she didn't come to the door. She wasn't in the apartment. I'm sure.
SUE: Did you ask her neighbors about her? You know, those people in the apartment above her. What's their name? Williams, I think.
MIKE: Yes, I did. I talked to their son . . . Bobby, I think his name is. He saw her yesterday morning. She ran in Washington Square Park, but he says she didn't come back. I mean, he didn't see her.
SUE: Really? Hmm. That's strange.
MIKE: Yes, it is. It's very strange. I . . . I can't understand it.

2 Answer these questions about the conversation.

1. Why is Mike calling Sue?
2. What did he and Jackie want to do last night?
3. When did Mike call Jackie?
4. Why is he worried about her now?
5. What did he do after he called her this morning?
6. Who did Mike talk to?
7. What did Bobby tell Mike?

3 Now ask and answer these questions.

1. When ___ Mike and Jackie have a date?
2. ___ Sue worried about Jackie too?
3. ___ Jackie in her apartment last night?
4. ___ Mike call her yesterday?
5. ___ he go to her apartment this morning?
6. ___ she there?
7. ___ she answer the door?

4 Open Dialog

Mike talked to Bobby Williams this morning.

What were his questions?

MIKE: _____?
BOBBY: Yes, I know her. I see her all the time.
MIKE: _____?
BOBBY: Yesterday? Yes, I saw her yesterday.
MIKE: _____?
BOBBY: When? Well, I saw her . . . uh . . . in the morning. She went out at seven. She ran in the park.
MIKE: _____?
BOBBY: When? Well, that's strange because she didn't come back. I mean, I didn't see her. And I always see her from my window.

16d

1 🎧 LISTEN

This building was a factory. But it isn't a factory now. People don't work here anymore.

It is in Greenwich Village, near a highway. The highway is behind the building. Can you see it?

There are four people in the old factory. One of the four is Jackie Hunter.

Jackie can't see the building. She doesn't know where she is. She can't see anything. There is a blindfold over her eyes.

She can't move her arms or legs. There are ropes around them. Jackie is tied to a chair. She can't stand up. She can't sleep. She can't talk.

But what happened yesterday? Why is Jackie in the old factory now?

Jackie left her apartment at seven. She ran in the park.

Lucky Jones and Frank Mitchum were there. They watched her. She didn't see them. When Jackie came back, they stopped her. Lucky had a gun. He and Frank had a van too.

"Don't scream. Don't talk. Don't run. Get into the van!" they told her.

Jackie got into the van. Lucky and Frank kidnapped her yesterday. That is why she isn't in her apartment now.

2 Ask and answer the questions.

Where is ....? Can Jackie ....?
When did ....?
Did Jackie ....? When did Lucky and Frank ....?

16e

1 🎧 LISTEN

This man is worried about Jackie too. He is Jackie's father and his name is Martin Hunter. He works in a bank, but he isn't a teller. He's the president. Mr. Hunter is a very rich man.

Mr. Hunter always works six days a week. He works from Monday to Saturday. He doesn't work on Sundays. On Sundays he usually gets up at seven thirty. Then he has breakfast. After that he reads the paper. And after that he works in his garden. He usually works for two or three hours. He starts at nine and finishes at eleven or twelve. Then he has lunch. He often plays golf in the afternoon. Sometimes he plays tennis. But he didn't do any of these things this morning or this afternoon. Harry Gilmore called him early this morning. And now Mr. Hunter is at San Francisco Airport. He is waiting for a plane to New York.

It is 10 A.M., Sunday morning, May 22.

2 Ask and answer questions about this man.

Who ....? Where ....? When does he usually ....?

Does he usually .... on Sundays? Did he .... { this morning? / this afternoon? }

3 Talk and write about the things Mr. Hunter usually does in the morning and in the afternoon.

He usually ...., but this { morning / afternoon } he didn't ....

4 Jackie often does these things on Saturdays. She didn't do them yesterday. Talk and write about them.

Example: She has breakfast.

She didn't have breakfast yesterday.

1. She listens to the radio.
2. She runs in the park.
3. She sees her friends.
4. She has lunch.
5. She studies.
6. She goes to Shakespeare's.
7. She writes her father a letter.

She didn't do other things yesterday. What were they?

5 What about you?

What do you usually do every day? Did you do these things last Sunday too?

Example: **I usually go to school/work every day, but I didn't go to school/work last Sunday.**

16f

1 And this is what Harry said to Mr. Hunter at seven o'clock this morning (San Francisco time). LISTEN

MR. HUNTER: Hello?
HARRY: Is this Mr. Martin Hunter?
MR. HUNTER: Yes. Who's this? What time is it? You woke me up!
HARRY: Listen to me, Mr. Hunter. I'm calling from New York. And I'm calling about your daughter.
MR. HUNTER: My daughter? Jackie? What's the matter? Is she . . . ?
HARRY: She's all right. We have her, Mr. Hunter.
MR. HUNTER: You have her? What do you mean? What is this? A joke?
HARRY: A joke? No, Mr. Hunter, it isn't a joke. I'm not laughing.
MR. HUNTER: I don't understand.
HARRY: Do you understand this? We kidnapped her Friday. And we want a million dollars.
MR. HUNTER: What? You . . . you what?
HARRY: Yes, I think you understand now. There's a plane from San Francisco to New York at eleven o'clock this morning. Get on that plane, Mr. Hunter. Get on it!
MR. HUNTER: And then? What then?
HARRY: There's a hotel in New York called the Park Hotel. I think you know it. Stay there and wait.
MR. HUNTER: Wait? Wait for what?
HARRY: My next phone call. At nine o'clock tomorrow morning. At the Park Hotel. That's all now.
MR. HUNTER: Wait! Stop! Who are you? What's your name? Hello? Hello?

2 Answer these questions about the conversation.

1. Where was Mr. Hunter when Harry called?
2. Does Mr. Hunter know Harry?
3. Does Mr. Hunter think this is a joke?
4. What does Harry want?

3 Read about Mr. Hunter.

It is ten o'clock in San Francisco now. It is Sunday.
Harry called Mr. Hunter at seven.
He is going to call him tomorrow too. He is going to call him at nine o'clock.
Mr. Hunter is in San Francisco now.
He is going to be in New York tonight.

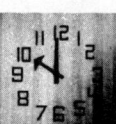
San Francisco Time

4 Now talk and write about Harry and Mr. Hunter.

1. Harry ___ going ___ call Mr. Hunter tomorrow.
2. Harry ___ ___ to call ___ nine o'clock.
3. Mr. Hunter ___ ___ ___ be in New York tonight.

5 Answer the questions.

1. Is Mr. Hunter going to get on a plane?
2. Which plane is he going to get on?
3. Is he going to stay at a hotel in New York?
4. Which hotel is he going to stay at?
5. What is he going to do at the hotel?
6. Harry wants a million dollars from him. Is he going to give Harry the million dollars? What do you think?

I think
I don't think } he is going to give ....

UNIT 17
The Telephone Call

17a

1

NEW YORK, SUNDAY MORNING

It is early in the morning. The sun is shining. It is going to be a warm day. But look at those clouds. Maybe it is going to rain.

2

IN THE FACTORY

Jackie can't sleep. Frank is sleeping in a chair near her. She is thinking.

JACKIE: What are they going to do to me? Am I going to see Mike, my father and my friends again? Or are they going to kill me? What am I going to do?

3

SAN FRANCISCO, SUNDAY MORNING

It is 11:00 A.M. at San Francisco Airport. A plane is taking off. It is flying to New York and Mr. Hunter is on it.
You can see another plane too.
It isn't taking off. It is going to take off.
It is going to take off in a minute.

4

ON THE PLANE

Mr. Hunter is going to smoke a cigarette. But first he wants to know something.

MR. HUNTER: When are we going to land in New York?
FLIGHT ATTENDANT: In five hours, sir.
MR. HUNTER: I mean, what time are we going to arrive there? New York time.
FLIGHT ATTENDANT: Seven o'clock, sir.

17b

1 Read about Mr. Hunter.

PICTURE ONE

1. What time is it in New York?
2. Do you think it is going to rain?
3. Is it raining now?
4. What kind of day do you think it is going to be?

It is twelve o'clock noon.
Mr. Hunter is flying to New York.
He is thinking about Jackie.
He is going to arrive in New York at seven o'clock New York time.
He is going to get there in four hours.
He is going to stay at the Park Hotel.
Harry is going to call him at nine o'clock tomorrow morning.

PICTURE TWO

1. What can you say about Jackie and Frank?
2. *Ask questions about her.*
   Are they going to ....?
   Is she going to ....?
3. What are some of the answers? What do you think?

2 Mr. Hunter is talking now. What is he saying?

I'm ____ing now.
I'm going to ....

3 Jackie usually does these things on Sunday. Is she going to do them today?

Ask and answer the question.

Is she going to ....?   No, she isn't.
                                   No, I don't think she is.
                                   No, I'm sure she isn't.

PICTURE THREE

1. Look at the two planes. What can you say about one of them?
2. What can you say about the other one?
3. What questions can you ask about Mr. Hunter?
   Is ....?
   Where ....?

1. She runs in Washington Square Park.
2. She takes a shower.
3. She eats a big breakfast.
4. She listens to the radio.
5. She reads the newspaper.
6. She has lunch with Mike.
7. She goes for a walk.
8. She sees her friends.

PICTURE FOUR

1. Is Mr. Hunter smoking a cigarette?
2. Is he going to smoke it?
3. What time is he going to arrive in New York?
4. What is his question?

17c

1 🎧 LISTEN

It is eight forty-five now. Marie and Tom Williams are still in bed. They usually get up at nine on Sundays.

Are they getting up now? Or are they going to get up?

Here are some other things they usually do on Sundays.

1. They have breakfast at nine thirty.
2. They read the Sunday paper.
3. They walk in the park before lunch.
4. They visit Marie's mother. She lives in another part of New York City.
5. Tom plays tennis in the afternoon.
6. After dinner they watch television.

Look at the pictures. Are they doing these things? Or are they going to do them?

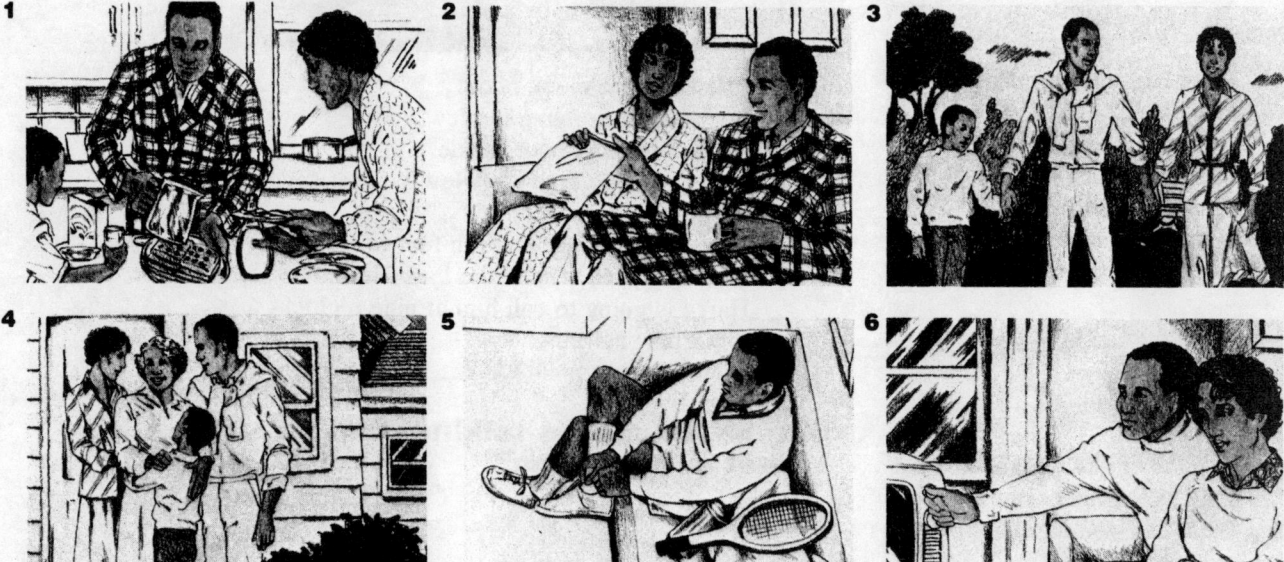

2 Look at the pictures again and ask and answer the questions.

| Is / Are | ___ | going to ___ ? |

or

| Is / Are | ___ | ___ing? |

Example:

PICTURE ONE: Are they having breakfast?   No, they aren't.
              Are they going to have breakfast?   Yes, they are.

3 What about you?

What do you usually do on Sundays?   I usually ....
What about next Sunday?   Next Sunday I think I'm going to ....

17d

1 Look at the pages from the calendar. 🔊

Today is Sunday, May 22.
Tomorrow is Monday, May 23.
The day after tomorrow is Tuesday.

Next week starts on Sunday, May 29.
Next month is June.

We can't see the year. What year is it now?
What about next year?

This is the calendar in the book.
But what about your calendar?

Look at your calendar. Then answer these questions.

1. What day is today?
2. What day is tomorrow?
3. And the day after tomorrow?
4. When does next week start?
5. What month is next month?
6. Talk about this year and next year:
   This year is 19—.
   Next year is 19—.

2 Jackie is in a factory in Greenwich Village today. Is she going to be there tomorrow too? She doesn't know. She is thinking. 🔊

JACKIE: Where am I now? What kind of place is this? I think it's a factory, but I'm not sure. Yes! It's probably a factory. Where am I going to be tomorrow? And the day after tomorrow? In this place? I hope not!

3 Jackie doesn't know where she is now. And she doesn't really know where she is going to be tomorrow.

But what about you?

    Tomorrow I'm going to be in ___.

    The day after tomorrow I think I'm going to be in ___.

    Next month I'm probably going to be in ___.

    I hope I'm going to be in ___ next year/the year after that/in 19—.

17e

1 It is nine o'clock Monday morning now. Harry is calling Mr. Hunter at the Park Hotel.

MR. HUNTER: Who are you? What's your name?
HARRY: You don't think I'm going to tell you that, do you?
MR. HUNTER: Where's my daughter? When am I going to see her again?
HARRY: Are you going to listen to me? Because if you aren't, I'm going to hang up.
MR. HUNTER: No. Don't hang up. I'm listening.
HARRY: We want a million dollars from you. Tomorrow. And . . .
MR. HUNTER: I know that. But I don't have a million dollars. Where am I going to find it?
HARRY: That's *your* problem. But if you want your daughter, find it.
MR. HUNTER: But I can't give you the money tomorrow. Give me more time.
HARRY: More time? How much more time? When can you give us the money?
MR. HUNTER: Probably the day after tomorrow.
HARRY: The day after tomorrow? No! We want the money tomorrow! And you're going to give us the money tomorrow—not the day after tomorrow! Do you understand?
MR. HUNTER: All right, all right! I'm definitely going to give you the money tomorrow.
HARRY: Definitely?
MR. HUNTER: Yes! Definitely!
HARRY: All right. I'm going to hang up now.
MR. HUNTER: Wait! When are you going to call again?
HARRY: Tomorrow. At three in the afternoon. Goodbye. That's all now.
MR. HUNTER: But . . . but . . . (Harry hangs up.)

2 Answer the questions.

1. What does Harry want?
2. Why can't Mr. Hunter give Harry the money today?
3. When can he give him the money?
4. Is he definitely going to do this or is he probably going to do this?
5. What is Harry going to do tomorrow?

3 Talk and write about Harry and Mr. Hunter.

1. Harry wants ___ ___ ___.
2. But Mr. Hunter can't ___ ___ ___ ___ today because ___ ___ ___ ___.
3. Harry ___ ___ ___ give him more ___.
4. Mr. Hunter is definitely ___ ___ ___ ___ ___ the day after tomorrow.
5. Harry ___ ___ ___ ___ ___ tomorrow ___ three o'clock in the ___.

4 Open Dialog

Lucky is asking Harry some questions. It is 10:00 Sunday morning.

LUCKY: _____?
HARRY: Yes, I did. I called him at nine o'clock.
LUCKY: _____?
HARRY: No, he can't give us the money today.
LUCKY: _____?
HARRY: Because he doesn't have it.
LUCKY: _____?
HARRY: Tomorrow.
LUCKY: _____?
HARRY: Yes, I am. Tomorrow. At 3:00.

17f

1 Look at the grammar: Future with GOING TO

I	am		be in the United States	on Friday.
He / She	is	going to	arrive in New York fly to Dallas	next week.
You / They / We	are		meet some friends play golf/tennis	at ___ o'clock.

Am	I		be in ___	on ___?		I	am.		I	'm not.
Is	he / she	going to	arrive in ___ fly to ___	next ___? at ___ o'clock?	Yes,	he / she	is.	No,	he / she	isn't.
Are	you / they / we		meet some ___ play			you / they / we	are.		you / they / we	aren't.

2 Read this about Carol Lee.

Last Monday Carol got up at seven o'clock, as usual. First she took a shower. Then she had breakfast. After that she walked to the station. Her train came at eight. She started work at nine and finished at five thirty as she always does.
On Mondays and Wednesdays Carol often meets some friends near Lincoln Center. They always meet at six and usually have dinner in an Italian restaurant. After that they usually go to a play or a concert.
It is Sunday night now and Carol is thinking about what she is going to do tomorrow.

3 Talk and write about Carol.

She is telling you what she is going to do tomorrow.
What is she saying?

1. Tomorrow/up/seven
2. Then/a shower
3. After that/breakfast
4. Then/the station
5. work/nine
6. five thirty
7. After work/some friends
8. We/a restaurant
9. After dinner/a concert

You don't know what Carol is going to do on Wednesday.
Ask her questions.

> Are you going to ....?
> Where/When are you going to ....?

1. your friends on Wednesday?
2. Where/dinner?
3. When/dinner?
4. a concert on Wednesday too?
5. Which concert?
6. When/concert start?
7. When/concert end?

4 What about you?

What are you **probably** going to do tomorrow?
What are you **definitely** going to do?

Can you write 6 sentences?

Tomorrow I am { probably / definitely } going to ....

102

UNIT 18
A Million Dollars!

18a

It is Monday morning, May 23. Jackie is still in a small room in a factory in Greenwich Village. Of course, she doesn't want to stay there. But she can't leave. She has to stay there. She has to sit in this chair. She can't get up. Frank has to stay in the room too. He has to watch her all the time.

Mike Brodsky has to get up early this morning. He has to take an examination today. He has to go to school. But he is thinking about Jackie.

MIKE: My God! I have to take an exam today. I have to answer a lot of questions. But how can I? Where's Jackie? Is she all right?

Mr. Hunter is thinking about Jackie too. And he is thinking about money.

MR. HUNTER: A million dollars! I have to find a million dollars! The kidnappers want it today. I have to find it before 3 o'clock. But how am I going to do that?

In another part of New York City, a man is having breakfast. He has to go to work soon. And he has a strange job. He has to wear those old clothes. Can you see them? People think he is a bum. But he isn't really a bum. He lives in a nice apartment. His name is Pat. Do you remember him? He is a detective.

18b

PICTURE ONE

1. What do you think Jackie wants to do?
2. Can she do it?
3. Why not?
4. *Talk about her and Frank.*
   She has to ....
   He has to ....

PICTURE TWO

1. What is Mike going to do today?
2. Do you think he wants to take the exam today?
3. Then why is he going to do it?
4. What is he thinking?

PICTURE THREE

Can you talk about Mr. Hunter too?

He has to ....

PICTURE FOUR

1. Who is this man?
2. What kind of job does he have?
3. What is his name?
4. He has to do strange things in his job. What are they?

1 Look at the grammar: HAVE TO

I We You They	have to	get up soon. go to work/school. take an exam. answer a lot of questions. find a million dollars.
He She	has to	

2 Talk and write about Carol.

Carol does these things every day. And she has to do them tomorrow.

Example: She gets up early.

She has to get up early tomorrow.

1. She walks to the station.
2. She takes a train to work.
3. She starts at nine.
4. She works seven and a half hours.
5. She does a lot of things.
6. She makes a lot of phone calls.
7. She types a lot of letters too.

3 Now Carol is talking to you. What is she saying?

I have to .... tomorrow.

4 What about you?

What do you have to do every day?
What do you have to do tomorrow?
What time do you have to .... tomorrow?

I have to .... every day.
I have to .... tomorrow.
Tomorrow I have to .... at ___ o'clock.

104

18c

1 🎧 LISTEN

It is almost three o'clock in the afternoon. Harry is going into a phone booth. What do you think he is going to do? Who do you think he is going to call?

What do you have to do when you make a phone call? Do you know?

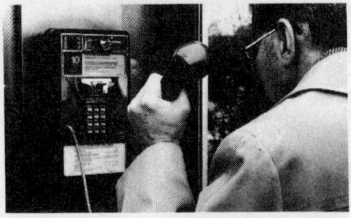  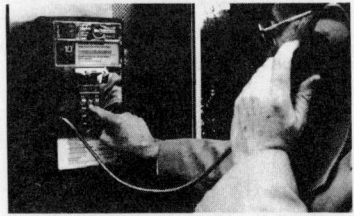

First, of course, you pick up the receiver.

Then you put some money in the slot.

After that you dial the number.

Do you understand all that? It's easy, isn't it?

Harry has a cassette player with him. He is going to play a cassette in a minute. What do you have to do when you play a cassette? Do you know?

First, of course, he is going to open the cassette player.

Then he is going to put in the cassette.

Then he is going to press the "play" button. Can you see that button? Is it on or off?

2 Talk and write about the telephone and the cassette player.

(a) What is Harry going to do in the phone booth?

First he is going to ....
Then ....
After that ....

(b) A friend from another country wants to use a telephone in the United States.

Tell your friend what he or she has to do.

First you **have to** ....
Then you **have to** ....
After that ....

(c) *Now tell a friend about the cassette player.*

What does he or she have to do first? And after that?

First you ___ to ___ the cassette player.
Then you ___ to ___ in the cassette.
After that ....

(d) What do you have to do when you record? Do you know?

18d

1 Now Harry is calling Mr. Hunter. LISTEN

HARRY: Do you have the money?
MR. HUNTER: Yes. What do I have to do now?
HARRY: Leave your hotel at seven o'clock tonight. Walk to Grand Central Station.
MR. HUNTER: Walk? Why do I have to walk?
HARRY: Shut up and listen! No questions. Put the money in a black briefcase. Do you understand? Then go to the waiting room at Grand Central. Be there at exactly seven forty-five.
MR. HUNTER: What do I have to do then?
HARRY: Go to the first telephone booth next to the door and wait. Stand in the booth.
MR. HUNTER: Wait a minute! How do I know my daughter is . . . I mean . . . maybe she's dead.
HARRY: Shut up and listen! I have a recording of her. Listen!
JACKIE: Hello, Dad. I don't know where I am, but I'm OK . . .
MR. HUNTER: Jackie? Jackie . . . !

2 Answer the questions.

1. Mr. Hunter has to do something at seven o'clock. What?
2. He has to go somewhere. Where?
3. What about the money? What does he have to do with it?
4. Where does he have to be at seven forty-five?
5. What does he have to do there?

3 Talk and write about Mr. Hunter.

1. At seven o'clock Mr. Hunter ___ to ___ the hotel.
2. He ___ ___ put the money in a ___ ___.
3. At seven forty-five he ___ ___ ___ to the waiting room at Grand Central Station.
4. He ___ ___ ___ in the first telephone booth next to the door.

18e

1 Mr. Hunter wants to know how to get to Grand Central Station. He is asking a clerk at the hotel. 🎧 LISTEN

MR. HUNTER: Can you tell me how to get to Grand Central Station?
CLERK: Yes, sir. It's on 42nd Street. You can take a taxi or a bus.
MR. HUNTER: No, no! I'm going to walk there.
CLERK: Oh, well. That's easy. We're on Central Park South. Go out of the hotel and turn right. Walk straight ahead to Fifth Avenue. Turn right on Fifth Avenue. Walk down Fifth Avenue to 42nd Street. Then turn left on 42nd Street. Grand Central Station is straight ahead. You can't miss it. It's on the left.

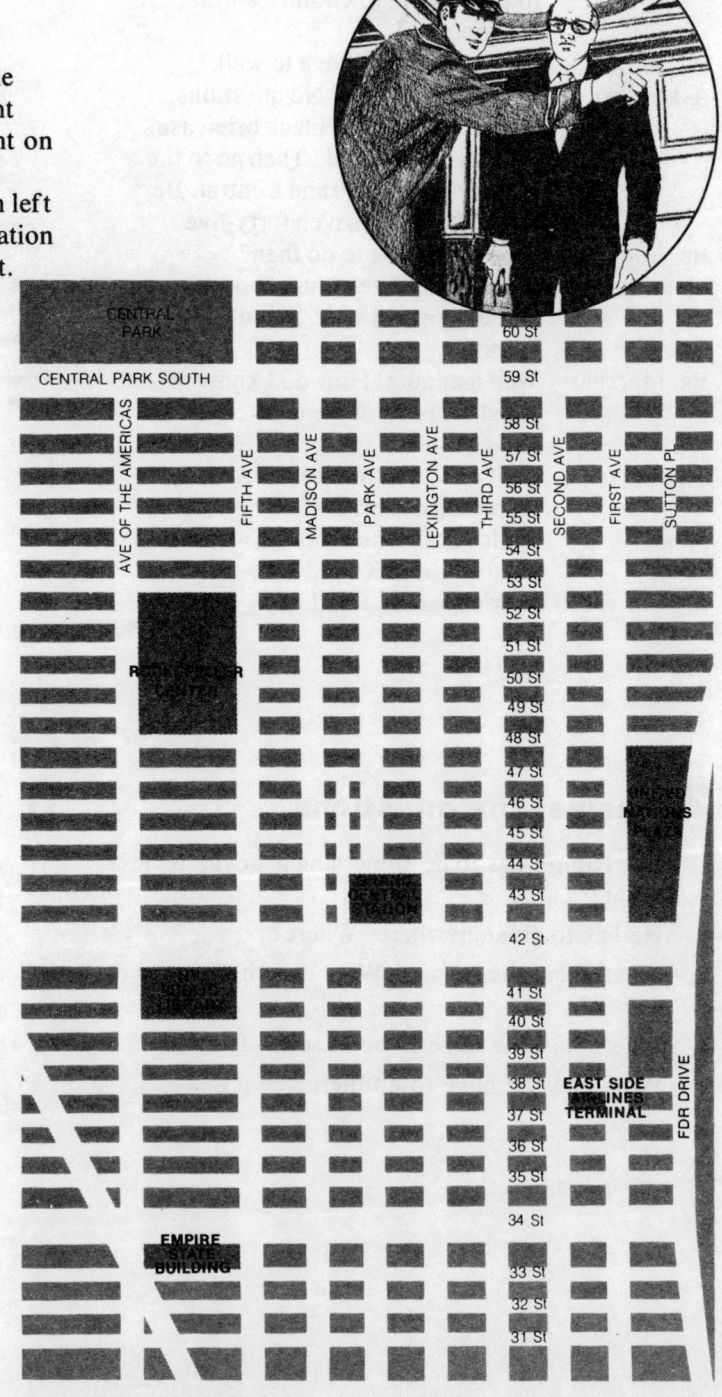

2 But can Mr. Hunter really remember all that? He is talking to himself. What is he saying?

MR. HUNTER: Now, let's see. When I ___ the hotel, I ___ right. Then I walk ___ ___ to Fifth Avenue. When I ___ ___ Fifth Avenue, I have to ___ ___. Then what? I can't remember.

Can you help him?

    Then you have to ....

3

You are at Grand Central Station. Someone is asking you how to get to these places. Can you tell him or her how to get to:

1. the airline terminal?
2. Rockefeller Center?
3. the New York Public Library?
4. the Empire State Building?
5. the United Nations?

    Turn right/left ....
    Walk down/up ....
    etc.

    OR

    You have to ....

18f

1 Look at the grammar: Questions and Answers with HAVE TO

> Mr. Hunter **has to leave** at seven.
> When **does** he **have to leave**?   At seven.

> I **have to leave** at seven.
> When **do** you **have to leave**?   At seven.

> He **has to go** to Grand Central Station.
> Where **does** he **have to go**?
>   To Grand Central Station.

> I **have to go** to Grand Central Station.
> Where **do** you **have to go**?
>   To Grand Central Station.

> He **has to walk** there.
> **Does** he **have to walk** there?   Yes, he **does**.

> I **have to walk** there.
> **Do** you **have to walk** there?   Yes, I **do**.

2 Let's talk about Carol again. She has to do these things every day. Do you remember?

1. She has to get up at seven.
2. She has to leave the house at 7:45.
3. She has to walk to the station.
4. She has to be there at eight.
5. She has to be at work at nine.

3 Open Dialog

You are asking Carol questions.

YOU: What time do you ___ to get ___?
CAROL: At seven.
YOU: And ___ ___ ___ ___ ___ ___ ___?
CAROL: Oh, at about seven forty-five.
YOU: ___ ___ ___ ___ ___ to the station?
CAROL: Usually.
YOU: And ___ ___ ___ ___ ___ ___ there?
CAROL: At eight o'clock. I always take the eight o'clock train.
YOU: ___ ___ ___ ___ have ___ be ___ ___?
CAROL: At work? At nine.

4 Now ask questions about her. What are the answers?

1. What ___ does ___ have to ___ ___?
   ___ seven.
2. ___ ___ she ___ ___ leave the ___?
   ___ 7:45.
3. ___ she ___ ___ walk to the ___?
   Yes, she ___.
4. ___ ___ ___ ___ ___ ___ ___ at the station?
   ___ eight.
5. Where ___ ___ ___ ___ ___ at nine?
   ___ ___ travel agency.

5 Complete these sentences.

What do you have to do every day? When do you have to do it?

1. I usually ___ ___ ___ up at ___.
2. On Mondays I ___ ___ ___ to work/school at ___ o'clock.
3. So I ___ ___ ___ the house at ___.

What are some other things you have to do on Tuesdays, Wednesdays, Thursdays or Fridays? Can you write about them?

   On ___ I usually have to ....

108

READING AND WRITING FOLLOW-UP: Units 16–18

Public Transportation in New York

If you want to travel by public transportation in New York, you can go by subway (an underground train) or by bus.

When you take the subway, you have to pay before you go down the stairs to the platform. The fare is always the same, but you can't use money to enter the subway. You have to buy a special "coin." It's called a *token*. You put the token in the turnstile (a kind of gate) and then you enter.

Subway Map

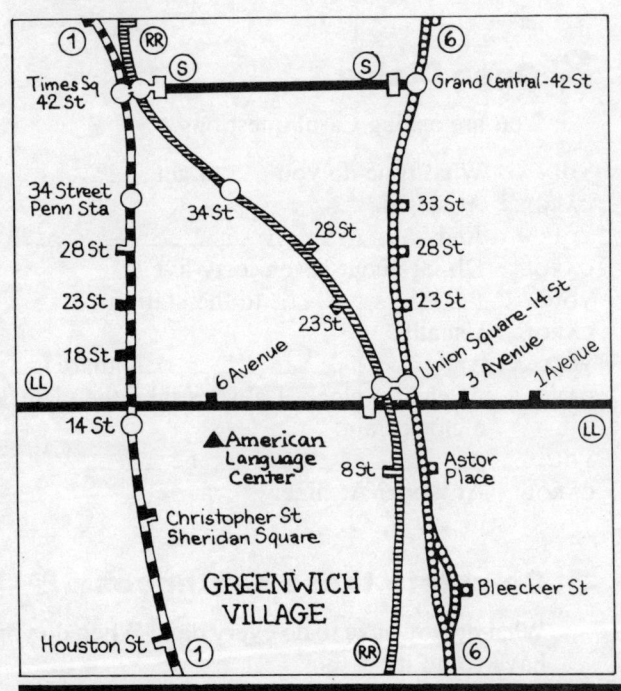

There are ten subway lines. There are local trains and express trains. Express trains don't stop at every station. At some stations you can change from the local train to the express train and at some stations you can change from one line to another.

During rush hour the subway trains are often full. Sometimes you can't get on a train and you have to wait for the next one. When people get on, they push and shove. You always have to stand. You can never get a seat.

The buses are crowded during rush hour too. Sometimes you can get a seat, but you usually have to stand. You pay when you get on the bus. You put your fare in a box next to the driver. The fares for the bus and the subway are the same. You can use money or a token on a bus. If you use money, you have to have the exact change.

Key to Subway Map

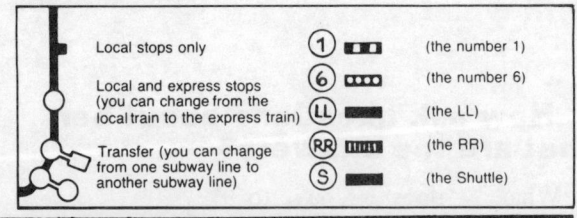

1 Talk and write about transportation in New York.

1. You live in New York, but your friend doesn't. Your friend is coming to visit you. Tell your friend about:
a) the two kinds of transportation.
b) the fare on the subway and the bus.
c) rush hour and what the people do, etc.

2. You live in Greenwich Village. Your friend is arriving at Grand Central Station. How can your friend get to Sheridan Square in Greenwich Village by subway? You are writing to him or her. What do you say? (Look at the subway map. For example: Take *the number 6/the Shuttle/the RR* to ___.)

   Take the ___ to ___. (Then change at ___.) Get off at ___.

3. Mario is a student in New York. He lives near 1st Avenue and he goes to the American Language Center in Greenwich Village. How does he travel by subway every day?

   He ___ the ___ to ___. Then he ___ at ___ and ___ to ___.

2 This is an advertisement for one of the museums in New York. Look at it. Then answer the questions.

1. What kind of things can you see in this museum?
2. You want to go to this museum, and you don't have a car. What do you have to do?
3. When can you see the exhibit?
4. Last Saturday you and a friend went to this museum. Write a postcard and tell another friend about it.

Dear _____,
Last Saturday _____ and I _____ the _____. We _____ the _____ to _____. Then we walked _____ museum. We _____ all the _____ there and it _____ very interesting.
See you soon.
_____

3 Which sentence goes with which picture?

a) You can't go out this way. Use the other door.
b) Don't do that! Use the trash can.
c) Hey! Don't go in there!
d) Stop! You're going into a one-way street.
e) Don't you know this is a no-smoking car?

4 Which signs go with which words?

1. Airport
2. Gentlemen
3. Do not enter
4. No smoking
5. Food served here
6. Telephone

 a   d
 b  e
 c   f

UNIT 19
Goodbye

19a

LISTEN

It is June now.
Flight 41 to San Francisco is going to leave soon.

LOUDSPEAKER: United Airlines announces the departure of Flight 41 to San Francisco. Passengers are requested to go to Gate 11 immediately, where this flight is now boarding.

Jackie is one of the passengers. She is saying goodbye to Mike.

JACKIE: Well, they're calling my flight now. I have to go.
MIKE: Goodbye, Jackie. See you soon.
JACKIE: Yes, Mike. Soon. Very soon.

Frank Mitchum is back in prison. He is sitting in a cell. And he is thinking.

FRANK: Here I am back in prison again. Why? Why did I listen to Lucky and Harry? Why didn't I find a job? My God! When am I going to get out of prison again? Maybe never! Am I going to die in this place?

And Harry? What about Harry? He is in prison too. He can't believe it.

HARRY: I can't believe it. I have to get up at six every morning. I have to wear this terrible uniform. I have to work every day. I can't drink. What happened? How did the police know?

19b

1 But what happened last month, on Monday, May 23? Why are Harry and Frank in prison now? Why isn't Lucky in prison too?

Read this and find out.

Mr. Hunter left his hotel at exactly seven o'clock. Pat was behind him. He followed Mr. Hunter to Grand Central Station. It was seven forty when Mr. Hunter got to the station. He went to the waiting room. Then he went into the first telephone booth next to the door. Harry called him at exactly seven forty-five. Mr. Hunter picked up the receiver and listened. Harry told him exactly what to do.

PICTURE ONE

1. What month is it now?
2. What can you see in the picture?
3. What are those people doing?
4. Where are they going?
5. What is the plane going to do?

2 Ask and answer questions about Mr. Hunter.

Example: What time ___ Mr. Hunter ___ his hotel?
What time did Mr. Hunter leave his hotel?
At exactly seven o'clock.

1. ___ Pat behind him?
2. ___ he ___ him to Grand Central Station?
3. When ___ they ___ to the station?
4. Where ___ Mr. Hunter ___ then?
5. What time ___ Harry ___ him?
6. What ___ Mr. Hunter ___ then?

PICTURE TWO

Ask and answer the questions.

1. Where ....?
2. Is Mike going to ....?
3. Is Jackie going to ....?
4. Does she have to ....?
5. Does he have to ....?

PICTURE THREE

1. Is Frank going to San Francisco too?
2. Where is he?
3. Do you think he is happy?
4. What are some of the things he is thinking?

3 You are Mr. Hunter. Talk and write about what you did that night last month.

PICTURE FOUR

You are talking to Harry.
Ask him questions.

1. ___ ___ happy?
2. Do you have to ....?
3. Can you ....?
4. Why do you have to ....?

19c

1 What did Harry tell Mr. Hunter to do?

MR. HUNTER: What do I have to do now?
HARRY: Go to the United Nations.
MR. HUNTER: The United Nations? Where's that?
HARRY: It's at the end of 42nd Street.
MR. HUNTER: Can I walk there?
HARRY: Yes, it's very near the station. When you go out of the station, turn left. Walk down the street. Stay on the left and stay near the curb. Don't cross the street. Do you understand?
MR. HUNTER: Go out of the station. Turn left. Don't cross the street. Walk down the street to the United Nations. Yes, I understand. What do I have to do when I get to the United Nations?
HARRY: Wait there! One more thing. Do the police know about this?
MR. HUNTER: Of course they don't.
HARRY: Good. Because if they *do,* you're never going to see your daughter again!
MR. HUNTER: Is she all right? When am I going to see her again?
HARRY: No more questions now. We want the money first. Do you have it?
MR. HUNTER: Of course I do.
HARRY: And is it in a black briefcase?
MR. HUNTER: Yes, it is. But . . .
HARRY: That's all for now. Goodbye.

2 Ask and answer these questions about Mr. Hunter.

It is Monday night, May 23.
It is seven forty-five.
What does Mr. Hunter have to do now?
Where does Mr. Hunter have to .... ?
Does he have to .... ?
What does he have to do when he .... ?

3 What do these words and phrases in the dialog mean?

Example: The United Nations? Where's *that?*
"that" = the United Nations

1. "Wait *there.*"
2. "Do the police know about *this?*"
3. "Of course they *don't.*"
4. "Good. Because if they *do,* you're never going to see your daughter again."

4 Answer these questions.

It is June now.
What did Mr. Hunter do that night last month?

First he left the hotel. Then he ___ to Grand Central Station. After that he ....
etc.

Mr. Hunter is telling you about that night last month. What is he saying?

MR. HUNTER: First I ___ my hotel. Then I ....
etc.

19d

1 And what happened then? Look at the pictures. Can you tell the story? 🎧 LISTEN

After Mr. Hunter left the station, he walked down 42nd Street. There was a lot of traffic. He stayed very near the curb.

But Mr. Hunter didn't walk to the United Nations. Before he got there, a man came up the street on a motorcycle. It was Lucky. He grabbed the briefcase from Mr. Hunter. And of course all the money was in the briefcase. Mr. Hunter didn't see Lucky's face. Lucky had a helmet on.

Pat was behind Mr. Hunter. Lucky didn't see him. But Pat saw Lucky. He didn't see his face either. But he saw the license number of the motorcycle. And he remembered it. Pat had a small radio in his pocket.

2 Ask and answer the questions.

Did ....?
Where was ....?
Why didn't ....?
What did ___ do?
Did ___ have a ___?

3 What do you think? What did Pat do with the radio?

Did he {
listen to Andrea Steele?
talk to the police?
talk to Mr. Hunter?
talk to Frank at the factory?
give the police the license number?
}

I'm sure he didn't ....
I think he probably ....
Maybe he ....

19e

1 And then what happened?

After Lucky grabbed the money, he drove to the old factory near the highway in Greenwich Village. But he didn't know that the police had his license number. You see, Pat called the police and gave them the number. He talked to them on his small pocket radio.

Three police cars followed Lucky. Of course, it was never the same police car. But one car was always in radio contact with the other two.

When Lucky got to the old factory, a policewoman saw him. She was in a building across the street. She had a small pocket radio too. Now the police knew exactly where Jackie was.

Twenty minutes later the police broke into the old factory. Frank was there. Harry and Lucky were there too. And of course, Jackie was there. The police freed her and arrested Harry and Frank. But they didn't arrest Lucky. Why not?

A minute before the police came, Lucky went to the bathroom. He was there when the police came. He heard them, of course. The bathroom was on the side of the factory next to another building. He climbed out of a small window, jumped onto the roof of the other building and then he ran away.

19f

1 You are a) Lucky Jones
   b) a policeman
   c) Pat
Tell your side of the story.

LUCKY: After I ...., I .... Then I .... When I was ...., the police .... They didn't .... because I ....

POLICEMAN: Three of our cars .... all the time. One of our policewomen .... Twenty minutes later we .... We arrested ...., but we didn't .... because ....

PAT: I .... Mr. Hunter. Lucky .... on a motorcycle and .... briefcase. I saw .... of the motorcycle. I .... on my pocket radio and they ....

2 What is going to happen to these people now? Read this and find out.

Jackie is going to come back to New York in September. She is going to live in Greenwich Village again. Mike isn't sure what he's going to do. Maybe he is going to find a job in Boston. Or maybe he is going to work in New York. He doesn't know. And Frank and Harry? They're going to be in prison for a long, long time!

And what about you? What are you going to do? Where are you going to be next year? Do you know?

3 Now talk and write about yourself.

Next month I'm going to ....
I'm going to .... next year.
I'm not sure/I don't know {what/where} I'm going to ....
I'm probably going to ....

REVIEW

Main *grammatical items* introduced appear in the structure tables.
Receptive items appear in the lists below the structure tables.

Unit 1

| What's (What is) your name? | My name's (is) Bill Rivera. |

| What time is it? | It's (It is) one o'clock. |

| Where's (Where is) | Los Angeles?
San Francisco? | It's in | the United States.
California. |

| Is | New York
San Francisco
Bill
Sue | in
from | the United States?
California? | Yes,
No, | it
he
she | is.
isn't. |

| Where | are you
is he/she | from? | I'm (I am)
He's (He is)
She's (She is) | from | Tokyo.
Buenos Aires.
Houston. |

This is New York.
San Francisco is **a city too.**
Thank you.
Nice to meet you.
Excuse me.
Look at Sue and Bill.
What about Sue?
Numbers 0–6.

Unit 2

| Where | is | Jackie
the taxi
Harry | going? | She
It
He | 's (is) | going **to** | the airport.
New York. |
| | are you | | | I'm (I am) | | | |

| Is | Harry
the taxi driver
Jackie
the plane | going to
coming from | New York? | Yes,
No, | he
she
it | is.
isn't. |

| Is | this
that | your | suitcase?
newspaper? | No, | this is
that's (that is) | my | suitcase.
newspaper. |

| I'm not (I am not)
Sue isn't (is not) | **at** the airport.
on the plane. |

Good morning.
She is in the taxi **now.**
Here you are.
Here's my ticket.
Put it right here, please.
Look at **this** man.
His name is Harry.
Okay. **Get in.**
Call **me** a taxi.
Numbers 7–18.

Unit 3

They're (They are)	near New York. in Boston. at South Station.

His Her	train	is on track four.
The train to New York		

What	time	is	the train to Rye?	11:45.
	track		it on?	Track 4.
How much			a one-way ticket to New York?	$19.50.

What's (What is)	he/she	doing?	I'm (I am) He's (He is) She's (She is) They're (They are)	buying	a ticket. coffee.
What are	you/they			running. talking.	

She is asking **about** the train to Rye.
Look at **that** woman.
Is this seat **taken?**
Numbers 19–65.

Unit 4

I You	can see	the Empire State Building. Jackie.

Can you see	that plane? the train?

We're (We are)	over New York landing	now.

Who's (Who is) this?	It's	Mike. the flight attendant.

She is talking to **him.**
No smoking, please.
Thanks.
Goodbye.
One picture is on the right. **The other** picture is on the left.

Unit 5

I You We They	have don't have	my your **our** their	cigarettes. suitcases. sweaters. car.
He She	has doesn't have	his her	umbrella toothbrushes. ticket.

118

Do	I you we they	have	a skirt? a pair of jeans? an umbrella? tickets	Yes,	I you we they	do.	No,	I you we they	don't.
Does	he she	have			he she	does.		he she	doesn't.

The hotel is	big. small. expensive. cheap.

The porter The policeman Jackie	is	waiting for looking at talking {to about}	her. him. them.

How many	suitcases boxes of cigars	do	you have?	I have	two. just one.

What do you have in	it? them?	Just	clothes. books.

She is walking **with** a porter.
Pat doesn't have a suitcase and he doesn't have a ticket **either**.
A policeman is looking at him, **but** he isn't looking at her.
How are you? Fine.
One of them is near Central Park. **The other** is near Grand Central Station.
The Park Hotel is **very** nice.
Do you have **these** things?
Here is Sue **again**.
The hotel is **between** a bar and a garage.
Which hotel is Jackie going to?
Numbers 70–150.

Unit 6

There	is isn't	a chair a sink	next to the door. in this room. in that hotel. over there.
	are aren't	two beds five windows	

Is	there	a shower a sink	in her room? in the bathroom?	Yes,	there	is. are.
Are		three beds four chairs	in this room? in his hotel?	No,		isn't aren't.

How many	beds chairs doors	are there in this room?	There	's only one.
				are four.

Can	you he Jackie the porters	see	them? the hotel? her?	Yes,	I he she they	can.
				No,		can't.

How long are you staying?
Are **those** your suitcases? Yes, they are./No, they aren't.
Is that all right? Yes, of course.
You're welcome.
Sure.
Certainly.
Two blocks from here.

Unit 7

I You He She	can can't	drive. type. dance. swim.

Can you play	tennis? the guitar?	Yes, I can, but not very well.

He can't speak **any** foreign languages.
Can you spell it, please?
Jackie is looking for an apartment **like** this.
And where is it? What's the address, **I mean**?

Unit 8

I You We They	**live work**	there. in that big building. in a hotel. **under us.**
He She	**lives works**	in the United States. **behind** the school.

Do	you they	**live** near a park? **teach** English? **speak** Chinese?	Yes, No,	I we they	**do. don't.**
Does	he she	**know** Jackie? **work** for the *Village News*?	Yes, No,	he she	**does. doesn't.**

It's **called** "Hello, Sun."
They live in the **same** building.
Do you **know** that name/her?

Unit 9

I You We They	always usually often sometimes*	get up at .... have breakfast at .... go to school/work at ....
He She		gets up at .... has breakfast at .... goes to school/work at ....

*Also: Sometimes I get up at ....

What time	do you	get up? have breakfast/lunch/dinner? go to work/school? get home? go to bed?
When	does he/she	

120

I think/I know she leaves at nine.
I don't know.
No, thanks. I don't smoke.
She .... **in the morning/on Monday/at ___/every day.**
Sometimes I don't have breakfast **at all.**
There are **some** books in that bookcase.

Unit 10

I You We They	**don't**	live in .... work in .... go to .... know .... own .... have lunch at ....
Mike Sue	**doesn't**	

Harry earns **a lot of** money.
He earns $100,000 **a** year.
I'm sure he's a burglar.
He wants **more.**
No more questions.

Unit 11

I	**want**	**some** carrots. a cup of coffee. a glass of wine. **some** soda.
He	**wants**	

She doesn't	**like**	the prisoners. pizza. mushrooms. steak. cold weather.
They don't		

I don't want **any**	beer. potatoes. ice cream.

Do you have any	fried rice? boiled potatoes? broiled fish? roast beef?

What kind of pizza do you want?
Do you want **anything else?**
Do you want anything **to drink?**
I'd/We'd like a pizza with peppers and mushrooms.
I **want to** pay for my dinner.

Unit 12

I You We They	want to	go to a movie. have a drink. go to the zoo. watch television. take a walk.
He She	wants to	

Let's	go to a movie. have a drink. go to the zoo. watch television. take a walk.

The fare to Greece is	$760	before after	September 15. July 1.

Where/when do they want to go?
The air fare is **more** in July, but it's **less** in March.
What else is playing?

Unit 13

I He She	was wasn't	at home in prison in Tokyo at school/work	yesterday. last month. last year. in 1979.
You We They	were weren't		

Was	Sue Frank I	tired hungry free in prison **outside** the school at a travel agency	this morning? last Thursday? at 10:00 yesterday? last night?	Yes, No,	she he I	was. wasn't.
Were	you we those men			Yes, No,	you we they	were. weren't.

Why	do you does he	want to	talk to see meet	me?	Because	I have he has	some money a job something	for you.

Simple Past: **followed, left, started, came, worked, went**

He started school **when** he was 5.
I/He **was born** in ....
That's why he's happy/she's smiling.

Unit 14

I / You / He / She / We / They	bought a newspaper / saw an ad / got the job / had pizza / earned $140 / studied math	yesterday. / on Monday. / last night. / last December. / last week. / last year.

Did	you / he / they	live / work	in	Cleveland / New York / Rye	last year? / before 1980? / after 1981?	Yes, / No,	I / he / they	did. / didn't.

What subjects did you study/like?
Do you mind if I ask you some questions?
It wasn't very **interesting**.

Unit 15

What time	did	you / she	get up / have lunch / go to work	yesterday?

What	did	you / Frank	say / eat / do	before / after	breakfast? / that? / you/he got home? / you/he went to school?

Someone wants to talk to you.
He left the house **at/about** midnight.
Are you **interested**?

Unit 16

I / You / He / She / We / They	didn't	go to a movie. / answer the phone. / have breakfast. / run in the park. / see any animals.

Why	didn't	you / she	go home? / see that movie?	Because ....

I / He	usually	get up at 7:30, have lunch at 12:30, / gets up at 9:00, has lunch at 1:00,	but	I / he	didn't	get up / have lunch	at .... this morning.

It's **almost** midnight.
Don't scream.
I **think/don't think** he's **going to** give me a million dollars.

123

Unit 17

I'm You're He's She's We're They're	going to	get there shave talk to Bobby fly to New York give them the money be in Boston	tomorrow afternoon. at nine o'clock. tonight. in a minute. next week. the day after tomorrow.

Tomorrow I think I'm going to ....
Next month I'm **probably** going to be in ....
I **hope** I'm going to be in .... next year.
She's **definitely** going to .... the day after tomorrow.

Unit 18

I You We The police	**have to**	get off here. get up early today. give Harry the money. pay the check. find Jackie.
Mr. Hunter Carol Lee	**has to**	

Do	I you we the police	**have to**	get off get up give it to him pay it find her	now?	Yes, No,	you I we they	do. don't.
Does	Mr. Hunter Carol Lee				Yes, No,	he she	does. doesn't.

Can you tell me **how to**	get to ....? use the telephone? record?	First . . . Then . . . After that . . .

Turn left/right.
Walk **straight ahead to/down** Fifth Avenue.
You can't miss it.

Unit 19 Review of *GOING TO* and the *Simple Past*.

DAYS, MONTHS, NUMBERS

DAYS OF THE WEEK

Sunday, Monday, Tuesday, Wednesday, Thursday, Friday, Saturday

MONTHS OF THE YEAR

January, February, March, April, May, June, July, August, September, October, November, December

NUMBERS

1 one	101 a hundred and one	1st first
2 two	102 a hundred and two	2nd second
3 three	160 a hundred and sixty	3rd third
4 four	200 two hundred	4th fourth
5 five	301 three hundred and one	5th fifth
6 six	484 four hundred and eighty-four	6th sixth
7 seven	1000 a/one thousand	7th seventh
8 eight	3,856 three thousand eight hundred and fifty-six	8th eighth
9 nine		9th ninth
10 ten		10th tenth
11 eleven		11th eleventh
12 twelve		12th twelfth
13 thirteen		13th thirteenth
14 fourteen		14th fourteenth
15 fifteen		15th fifteenth
16 sixteen		16th sixteenth
17 seventeen		17th seventeenth
18 eighteen		18th eighteenth
19 nineteen		19th nineteenth
20 twenty		20th twentieth
21 twenty-one		21st twenty-first
22 twenty-two		22nd twenty-second
30 thirty		30th thirtieth
40 forty		40th fortieth
50 fifty		50th fiftieth
60 sixty		60th sixtieth
70 seventy		70th seventieth
80 eighty		80th eightieth
90 ninety		90th ninetieth
100 a/one hundred		100th hundredth

VERB LIST WITH PAST TENSE FORMS

Parentheses indicate that the form is not used in the text. Irregular present forms are also given.

Verb	Regular	Irregular	Verb	Regular	Irregular
address	addressed		buy		bought
announce	(announced)		call	called	
answer	answered		can—can		(could)
apply—applies	(applied)		carry—carries	(carried)	
arrest	arrested		change	(changed)	
arrive	(arrived)		choose		(chose)
ask	asked		climb	climbed	
be—am, are is,		was, were	close	(closed)	
believe	(believed)		come		came
board	(boarded)		complete	(completed)	
break		broke	cook	(cooked)	
bring		(brought)	cost		(cost)
burn	burned		cross	(crossed)	

Verb	Regular	Irregular	Verb	Regular	Irregular
dance	(danced)		play	(played)	
dial	(dialed)		prefer	(preferred)	
dictate	(dictated)		press	(pressed)	
die	(died)		put		(put)
do—does		did	rain	(rained)	
drink		drank	read		read
drive		drove	record	(recorded)	
earn	earned		remember	remembered	
eat		ate	request	requested	
end	ended		return	returned	
enter	(entered)		ring		(rang)
excuse	(excused)		run		ran
find		found	say		said
finish	finished		scream	(screamed)	
fly—flies		(flew)	see		saw
follow	followed		send		(sent)
free	freed		serve	(served)	
get		got	set		(set)
give		gave	share	(shared)	
go—goes		went	shave	shaved	
grab	grabbed		shine		(shone)
hang		(hung)	shove	(shoved)	
happen	happened		shut		(shut)
have—has		had	sign	signed	
hear		heard	sing		(sang)
help	(helped)		sit		sat
hope	(hoped)		sleep		slept
hurry—hurries	(hurried)		smile	(smiled)	
include	(included)		smoke	(smoked)	
interview	interviewed		snow	(snowed)	
jump	jumped		speak		(spoke)
kidnap	kidnapped		spell	(spelled)	
kill	(killed)		stand		(stood)
knock	knocked		start	started	
know		knew	stay	stayed	
land	(landed)		steal		(stole)
laugh	(laughed)		stop	stopped	
learn	(learned)		study—studies	studied	
leave		left	swim		(swam)
let		(let)	take		took
lift	(lifted)		talk	talked	
like	liked		teach		(taught)
listen	listened		tell		told
live	lived		thank	(thanked)	
look	looked		think		thought
make		(made)	travel	(traveled)	
manage	managed		turn	turned	
mean		(meant)	type	typed	
meet		met	understand		(understood)
mind	(minded)		use	used	
miss	(missed)		visit	(visited)	
move	(moved)		wait	waited	
open	(opened)		wake		woke
order	(ordered)		walk	walked	
park	(parked)		want	wanted	
pay		(paid)	watch	watched	
pick	picked		wear		(wore)
			work	worked	
			write		(wrote)

WORD LIST

The numbers after each word indicate the page number where the word first appears.

adj = adjective; *adv* = adverb; *aux* = auxiliary verb; *conj* = conjunction; *interj* = interjection; *n* = noun; *prep* = preposition; *pron* = pronoun; *v* = verb

a

a 2
about *prep* 14
  adv 86
  what about? 3
above *prep* 93
accommodations 69
across *prep* 53
actor 66
actress 66
ad (=advertisement) 49
add 69
address *n* 30
  v 69
advertisement 49
after *prep* 49
  conj 84
afternoon 13
again 17
agency 49
  travel agency 31
agent
  ticket agent 7
  travel agent 69
ahead
  go ahead 88
  straight ahead 107
air *adj* 67
air-conditioned *adj* 69
airline 15
  airline terminal 107
airport 5
alarm clock 26
alcohol 89
all *pron* 32
  all right 23
  first of all 67
  not at all 44
almost 91
also 4
always 43
am *v* 4
  aux 7
A.M. 95
American *adj* 32
  American Plan 69
an 17
and 2
animal 59
announce 15
announcement 15

announcer 15
another *adj* 86
  pron 109
answer *v* 2
  n 26
any *adj* 32
anymore 94
anything 60
apartment 35
  apartment building 37
apple pie 62
apply 89
appointment book 85
are *v* 4
  aux 7
arm *n* 94
around *prep* 94
arrest *v* 115
arrival 15
arrive 15
article 51
as *conj* 85
  as usual 102
ask 2
assistant 90
at 2
attendant
  flight attendant 13
  parking lot attendant 90
avenue 2
away
  run away 115
  take away 54

b

back
  come back 91
  go back 73
bacon 26
bad 61
bag 6
baked *adj* 62
ballet 61
bank *n* 43
bar *n* 21
bartender 90
bath 29
bathroom 23
bay 70

be *present* 1
  past 71
  command 106
  be born 75
beach 69
beans 59
beautiful 70
because 71
bed 23
bedroom 35
beef 12
beer 12
before *prep* 68
  conj 77
  adv 88
behind *prep* 37
believe 111
best 69
between *prep* 21
beverage 62
big 9
bill *n* 30
black 106
blindfold 94
block *n* 28
blood 65
blouse 18
board *v* 111
boiled *adj* 59
book *n* 6
  appointment book 85
bookcase 46
booth: phone booth 105
born: be born 75
boss *n* 40
bottle 18
boutique 90
box *n* 90
boy 39
boyfriend 61
bread 31
break into 115
breakfast 26
bridge *n* 65
briefcase 6
bring 19
brochure 67
broiled *adj* 59
brother 29
building 2
  apartment building 37
bum 103
burglar 51
burn *v* 65
bus 27
  by bus 109
busy 87
but 21

butter *n* 59
button *n* 105
buy 9
by
  by bus 109
  by subway 109
  by train 87
bye (=goodbye) 43

c

cafeteria 45
cake: cheese cake 62
calendar 71
calf 59
call *v* 7
  phone call *n* 88
camera 6
can *aux* 4
car 17
carrot 59
carry 17
carton 18
cassette 105
  cassette player 105
cell 111
cent 9
center *n* 32
certainly 28
chair 23
change *v* 109
charge: service charge *n* 69
cheap 21
check *n* 30
cheese 12
cheese cake 62
chicken 59
children 29
Chinese *n* 34
  adj 86
chocolate 62
choose 4
cigar 13
cigarette 11
city 2
class *n* 32
  first class 69
classroom 24
clean *adj* 49
clerk 7
climb *v* 86
  climb out of 115
clock: alarm clock 26
  o'clock 1
close *v* 88
closed *adj* 89
clothes 22

127

cloud 97
club 55
   nightclub 55
coat *n* 6
coffee 11
   coffee shop 26
coin 109
Coke 11
cold 57
color 69
come 5
   come back 91
   come on 37
comedy 65
complete *v* 4
concert 85
contact: in radio contact 115
conversation 4
cook *v* 33
   n 89
corner *n* 29
cost *v* 29
country 3
couple 67
course: of course 23
court: tennis court 69
cow 59
cowboy 31
cross *v* 113
crowded *adj* 109
cup 57
curb *n* 114

d

Dad 28
dance *v* 33
date *n* 50
daughter 96
day 41
dead 41
dear 27
definitely 101
degree 90
delicious 61
deluxe 69
departure 29
dessert 62
destination 10
detective 103
dial *v* 105
dictate 51
did *aux* 78
die *v* 111
different 50
dinner 45
disaster 65
disc jockey 37
disco 69
divorced *adj* 29
do *v* 10
   aux 17

dollar 9
door 23
dormitory 49
double *n* 23
   double room 30
down *prep* 107
   down there 13
   sit down 83
dress *n* 18
drink *n* 31
   v 55
drive *v* 33
driver
   driver's license 90
during 109

e

early 95
earn 55
east 90
easy 69
eat 26
egg 26
   egg salad 12
either *adv* 19
elevator 25
else
   anything else? 60
   what else? 66
enclosed *adj* 50
end *v* 51
engineer 40
engineering *n* 61
English *n* 32
enter 109
entrance 110
entree 62
envelope 70
etc. (=et cetera) 75
European Plan 69
evening 45
   good evening 23
ever 59
every 43
everybody 43
exact 109
exactly 51
exam/examination 103
example 92
excellent 61
excuse me? 4
   excuse me 11
exhibit *n* 110
exit 110
expensive 21
experience *n* 90
express *adj* 109
eye 94

f

face *n* 114
factory 40
fair *adj* 70
family 29
fare 10
father 27
favorite 37
few *adj* 70
fiction: science fiction 65
fifth *adj* 2
filet of sole 62
find *v* 54
   find out 112
fine *adj* 19
finish *v* 43
finished *adj* 60
first *adj* 37
   adv 97
   first class 69
   first of all 67
fish 59
   tuna fish 12
flight 15
   flight attendant 13
floor 25
fly *v* 32
follow 25
food 31
for 17
   for now 54
foreign 32
form *n* 50
fourth *adj* 53
free *adj* 69
   v 115
   tax free 90
French *n* 34
   french fries 62
fried *adj* 59
friend 17
friendly 50
from 3
front: in front of 91
fruit 31
full 70
   full-time 50
furnished *adj* 49

g

garage 21
garden *n* 95
gate 29
gentlemen 110
get 31
   get home 45
   get in 7
   get into 94
   get off 87
   get on 87
   get out 81

   get to 69
   get up 26
girlfriend 62
give 51
glass 58
go 5
   go ahead 88
   go back 73
   go in 91
   go on 84
   go out 83
God
   thank God 61
   My God! 103
going to (+*v*) 96
golf 95
good *interj* 11
   adj 34
   good morning 5
   good evening 23
goodbye 13
grab 114
grammar 4
guard *n* 71
guest 30
guitar 20
gun 22

h

had 79
half *adj* 69
ham 12
hand *n* 57
hang up *v* 101
hangout 89
happen 94
happy 61
hard *adv* 89
has/have *v* 17
   has to/have to *aux* 103
hat 17
he 3
hear 15
heavy 22
hello 1
helmet 114
help *v* 19
her *adj* 9
   pron 17
here 5
   here is 7
   over here 19
   right here 7
hey 1
hi 1
highway 94
him 13
himself 89
his *adj* 7
history 81
holiday 69
home 45

128

hope *v* 70
horror *adj* 65
horse 27
hot 70
hotel 7
hour 49
   rush hour 109
house *n* 32
how
   how are you? 19
   how long? 25
   how many? 22
   how much? 9
   how old? 76
hungry 57
hurry *v* 53
husband 37

i

I 4
ice cream 62
if 81
immediately 111
in 2
include 69
information 31
interested *adj* 88
interesting *adj* 79
international 90
interview *n* 81
   v 84
into 83
irregular 80
is *v* 1
   aux 5
it 1
Italian *n* 34
   adj 50

j

jacket 86
Japanese *n* 50
jazz 49
jeans 18
jelly 58
job 31
jockey: disc jockey 37
joke *n* 96
juice 26
jump *v* 115
just *adv* 11

k

key 25
kid *n* 88
kidnap 94
kidnapping *n* 91

kill *v* 97
kind *n* 57
kitchen 35
knock *v* 93
know (+*n*) 39
   (+*clause*) 45

l

lake 27
lamb 59
land *v* 13
language 32
last *adj* 50
late 9
later 65
laugh *v* 65
law 43
learn 32
leave *v* 11
lecture *n* 51
left: on the left 15
leg 94
less *adj* 67
let's (+*v*) 57
letter 26
library 45
license
   driver's license 90
   license number 114
lift *v* 32
light *n* 26
like *prep* 31
like *v* 50
   I'd like 60
limit *n* 85
line: subway line 109
listen 1
   listen to 19
live *v* 29
living room 35
local 89
location 49
long *adj* 90
   how long? 25
look *v* 5
   look at 2
   look for 35
lot
   a lot *adv* 57
   a lot of *n* 50
lot: parking lot 17
loudspeaker 111
love *n* 27
lunch *n* 42

m

machine 85
magazine 84
mailbox 28
make *v* 89
male *adj* 49

man *n* 9
   interj 22
manage 77
manager 34
many *adj* 89
   how many? 22
map 3
married *adj* 29
math 81
matter: what's the matter? 91
maybe 67
me 4
meal 49
mean *v* 34
meat 31
mechanic 50
medicine 50
meet *v* 1
menswear 90
menu 12
midnight 26
mile 90
milk *n* 11
million 96
mind *v* 81
minute *n* 28
miss *n* 11
   Miss *n* 26
miss *v* 107
moderate *adj* 69
Mom 27
money 55
month 36
more *adj* 55
   pron 55
   no more 54
morning 26
   good morning 5
mother 27
motorcycle 114
move *v* 94
movie 30
   movie theater 31
Mr. 27
Mrs. 27
Ms. 70
much
   how much? 9
   too much *adj* 89
   very much *adv* 50
museum 110
mushroom *n* 57
music 37
my 1
   My God! 103

n

name *n* 1
named *adj* 77
nation 27
near *prep* 11
necessary 90

neighbor 86
never 46
new 41
news 49
newspaper 6
next *adj* 34
next to *prep* 23
nice 28
   nice to meet you 1
night 21
nightclub 55
ninth *adj* 51
no 2
noise 89
non-smoker 49
noon 51
not 2
note: take notes 51
now 5
   for now 54
number *n* 8
   license number 114

o

o'clock 1
of 18
   of course 23
off 105
   get off 87
   take off 97
office 40
   post office 28
often 45
oh *interj* 4
OK 7
old 17
   how old? 76
on *prep* 5
   adj 105
   get on 87
   go on 84
one *adj* 15
   pron 19
   one way 9
only 23
onto 115
open *v* 71
operator 26
opportunity 90
or 4
orange 26
order *v* 60
   to the order of 30
organization 90
other *adj* 15
   pron 21
out 73
   climb out of 115
   come out 83
   find out 112
   get out 81
   go out 83

outside *prep* 71
over *prep* 13
   over here 19
   over there 28
own *adj* 49
   v 51
owner 36

p

pack *n* 92
package 69
page *n* 85
pair *n* 18
paper (=newspaper) 66
parents 29
park *n* 21
park *v* 17
parking lot 17
   parking lot attendant 90
part *n* 31
   part-time 50
partner 4
passenger 17
pay *v* 23
   pay for 57
peas 59
pen pal 50
people 20
pepper 57
per 69
perfume 18
person 23
   in person 90
phone (=telephone) *n* 26
   phone booth 105
   phone call 88
photograph *n* 55
phrase *n* 113
pick up 105
picture *n* 2
pie 62
pizza 57
place *n* 89
plan
   American Plan 69
   European Plan 69
plane 5
platform 9
play *v* 33
   play button 105
player: cassette player 105
please 5
plus *prep* 30
P.M. 85
pocket *n* 86
police *n* 53
policeman 27
policewoman 17
pool: swimming pool 70
popular 89
porter 7
post office 28

postcard 27
potato 59
prefer 49
president 43
press *v* 105
price 23
prison 57
prisoner 57
private 30
probably 100
problem 49
program *n* 37
public *adj* 107
purse *n* 85
put 7

q

question *n* 2
quiet 89

r

radio 37
   in radio contact 115
rain *v* 13
raincoat 20
raw 59
read *v* 26
really? 4
receiver 105
record *n* 37
   v 105
recording *n* 106
red 60
refrigerator 35
registration 50
regular 80
remember 44
rent *n* 36
reporter 40
request *v* 111
reservation 23
restaurant 29
return *v* 85
review *n* 14
rice 59
rich 43
right *adj* 16
   all right *adj* 23
   on the right *adv* 15
   right here *adv* 7
ring *v* 26
road 70
roast *adj* 12
rock and roll 85
roof 115
room 21
   Room Service 26
   waiting room 106
rope 94

round trip 9
row *n* 85
run *v* 9
   run away *v* 115
rush hour 109

s

salad 57
   egg salad 12
salary 79
sales 90
   sales assistant 90
salesperson 90
same 37
sandwich 12
say *v* 4
school 32
science fiction 65
scotch 18
scream *v* 94
seat *n* 11
second *adj* 29
secretary 40
see 1
send 50
sentence *n* 8
separate *adj* 49
serve *v* 89
service
   Room Service 26
   service charge 69
set *v* 26
share *v* 49
shave *v* 83
she 3
sheriff 65
shine *v* 37
shirt 18
shoe 22
shop: coffee shop 26
short 69
shove *v* 109
shower *n* 23
   take a shower 83
shut up 106
side 115
sign *v* 23
   n 89
signature 50
sincerely 50
   sincerely yours 69
sing 46
single *n* 23
   adj 29
sink *n* 23
sir 7
sirloin 62
sister 29
sit 46
   sit down 83
sixth *adj* 37
sleep *v* 63

slot 105
small 21
smile *v* 71
smoke *v* 13
   non-smoker 49
snack bar 11
snow *v* 61
so: I think so 47
soda 12
sole 62
some *adj* 45
someone 88
something 76
sometimes 44
somewhere 106
son 39
soon 61
sorry 19
south 107
Spanish *n* 34
speak 32
special 109
spell 36
sports 49
square 30
staff *n* 90
stairs 25
stamp *n* 27
stand *v* 27
   can't stand 61
   stand up 94
star *n* 65
start *v* 34
state *n* 2
station 9
stay *v* 25
steak 57
steal 51
stereo 46
still *adv* 63
stop *v* 70
store *n* 30
story 65
stove 35
straight ahead 107
strange 93
street 2
strong 32
student 24
studio 49
study *v* 50
subject *n* 81
subway 109
   subway line 109
sugar 11
suit *n* 18
suitable 49
suitcase 5
sun 37
supermarket 31
sure *adv* 23
   adj 53
sweater 18

t

swim *v* 33
swimming pool 69

table 35
take *v* 19
   take a shower 83
   take away 54
   take off 97
taken *adj* 11
talk *v* 7
tax *n* 30
   tax free 90
taxi 5
tea 12
teach 32
teacher 24
telephone *n* 26
television 45
tell 36
teller 95
tennis 33
   tennis court 69
terminal: airline terminal 107
terrace 49
terrible 57
thank
   thank God 61
   thank you 1
   thanks 13
that *pron* 5
   adj 10
the 2
theater 30
   movie theater 31
their 17
them 19
then 44
there 13
   there is/are 23
these *adj* 18
they 9
thing 18
think 45
third *adj* 29
this *pron* 2
   adj 7
those *pron* 25
thousand 55
through *prep* 53
ticket *n* 5
   ticket agent 8
tied *adj* 94
time

full-time 50
part-time 50
on time 91
what time? 1
tired *adj* 26
to 1
toast *n* 26
today 31
toilet 23
token 109
tomorrow 100
tonight 41
too 1
   too much 89
toothbrush 18
top *adj* 49
total *n/adj* 30
tour 69
tourist 50
town 41
track 15
traffic 114
train 9
   by train 87
transit 110
transportation 49
travel *adj* 31
   v 109
   travel agency 31
   travel agent 69
tree 27
trip *n* 90
   round trip 9
tuna fish 12
turn *v* 107
   turn on 37
turnstile 109
type *v* 34

u

umbrella 17
under 39
underground 109
understand 53
unhappy 83
uniform *n* 111
university 43
up *adv* 25
   prep 107
   up there 13
us 39
use *v* 70
usual 81
   as usual 102
usually 45

v

vacation 69
vampire 65
van 94
vanilla 62
veal 59
vegetables 31
verb 80
very 21
view *n* 70
village 31
visit *v* 109
vocabulary 90

w

wait *v* 36
   wait for 17
waiter 12
waiting room 106
waitress 75
wake up 96
walk *v* 17
   n 98
want (+*n*) *v* 57
   want to (+*v*) 50
wanted *adj* 79
war 65
warm *adj* 61
was *v* 71
watch *v* 37
water *n* 60
way
   on the way 70
   one way 9
we 13
wear *v* 17
weather 49
week 43
welcome: you're welcome 26
well *interj* 13
   adv 33
were *v* 71
west 90
western *n* 31
what? 1
   conj 59
   what a (+*n*!) 84
   what about? 3
   what else? 66
   what kind? 57
   what time? 1
when? 45
   conj 75
where? 3
   where to? 5

which? 21
who? 16
why? 72
   conj 71
wife 51
window 23
wine 60
with 17
without 29
woman 9
wonderful 61
word 34
work *v* 40
   n 41
worried *adj* 91
write 4
wrong 18

y

yeah 22
year 55
yes 1
yesterday 71
you 1
young 67
your 1
yourself 50

z

zoo 63